W9-DGY-479

CHICAGO PUBLIC LIBRARY
HAROLD WASHINGTON LIBRARY CENTER

R0007237365

YM
139
.R6
1974
cop. 1

FORM 125 M

APPLIED SCIENCE &
TECHNOLOGY DEPARTMENT

The Chicago Public Library

Received_____ JUL 3 1975 _____

THE CHICAGO
PUBLIC LIBRARY

FOR REFERENCE USE ONLY
Not to be taken from this building

ALSO BY BILL ROBINSON

The Science of Sailing
(editor)

New Boat

A Berth to Bermuda

Where the Trade Winds Blow

Expert Sailing

Over the Horizon

The World of Yachting

Better Sailing for Boys and Girls

The Best from Yachting
(editor)

The America's Cup Races
(coauthor)

Legendary Yachts

The Sailing Life

The Right Boat for You

The Great American Yacht Designers

Overleaf: Nathanael Herreshoff's Thistle, *built in 1928, is still sailing in the Aegean.*

Bill Robinson

The Great American Yacht Designers

Alfred A. Knopf   New York   1974

REF
VM
139
.R6
1974

Cop. 1

THIS IS A BORZOI BOOK
PUBLISHED BY ALFRED A. KNOPF, INC.

Copyright © 1970, 1971, 1972, 1974, by Bill Robinson

All rights reserved under International and Pan-American Copyright Conventions.
Published in the United States by Alfred A. Knopf, Inc., New York,
and simultaneously in Canada by Random House of Canada Limited, Toronto.
Distributed by Random House, Inc., New York.

Some of this material appeared in a slightly different form in *Yachting* Magazine.

Library of Congress Cataloging in Publication Data

Robinson, William Wheeler   date   The great American yacht designers.
Contents: The lonely profession.—Nathanael Herreshoff.—Clinton Crane.—John Alden. (etc.)
1. Yacht-building. 2. Yachts and yachting—United States.   I. Title.
VM139.R6   1974   623.82'02'0922   74-7746
ISBN 0-394-42721-1

Manufactured in the United States of America
First Edition

THE CHICAGO PUBLIC LIBRARY
JUL 3 1975

Contents

TEC
Ref

The Great American
Yacht Designers

One

The Lonely Profession

The very special trade of designing yachts is one of the most individualistic there is. It is less bound by precise qualifications and routines than almost any other profession dealing with such practical factors as engineering details and mathematical formulas. Despite this relationship to engineering and technical matters, yacht designing is such an individualistic métier that it could almost be compared to playwriting, or perhaps sculpture. What makes a great playwright? Or sculptor? Certainly an intangible, a spark that has nothing to do with education, background, or station in life. Thousands of students have taken courses in creative writing or have gone to art classes without turning out one memorable piece of drama or sculpture.

Fewer young hopefuls, by thousands, have aspired to become yacht designers. However, there have been a great many students passing through courses in naval architecture and related subjects at the small number of institutions offering them whose names have never been heard by anyone outside their private circle. And there have been some designers, in fact many of the best, who have had very little formal training before achieving fame.

Over the past century only a handful of men have left a noticeable mark on this lonely profession, and, true to the lack of any specific pattern or formula for success, they have done it in very different ways. Each one is always very much on his own in the pursuit of this career. The lines of conduct, the specifications and requirements for being a yacht designer, have never been laid out precisely or been codified in any way, and it is indeed a profession that has had a topsylike growth. Its beginnings go back to a day when designing a boat was very definitely a form of sculpture. It was done in solids, not on paper, and it took an "eye" and a feel that could not be defined.

When yachting began to emerge in the early nineteenth century as a specialized form of marine activity for leisure hours, as opposed to the well-established pursuit of serious seafaring in commerce and warfare, its vessels were derived and adapted from commercial models, such as pilot schooners and fishing smacks. These traditional types had evolved over centuries of use, and hull forms and rigs were a combination of minor innovations with practices that were followed because "Things had always been done that way." The "art" of shipbuilding, for that's what it was, was handed down from generation to generation by the actual doing, by apprenticeship and gradual development of knowledge.

When someone had a new idea for the form a hull should take, he would carve out that form in a small model, and the model's lines would then be adapted to the full-sized vessel. Among the early yachtsmen, John Cox Stevens, first commodore of the New York Yacht Club (NYYC) when it was formed in 1844, had since early youth designed his own yachts by carving models of them and presenting them to a builder for adaptation to full size. The schooner *America*, whose syndicate he headed, was built by William Brown in a yard on New York's East River from a model carved by a young designer named George Steers. Working with Stevens, Steers adapted the lines of the swift pilot schooners to racing-yacht use; this one boat and her familiar story had perhaps the single most important effect on the development of the sport, and on the evolution of yacht designing as a special profession. It was through designing America's Cup yachts that most of the early designers came to fame. Before long, there was an opportunity for someone with some ideas and some feeling for innovations to show his wares in the America's Cup programs.

There are not many names that come down from the early years of yachting, and, right up until modern times, there have been very few yacht designers practicing at the same time. Never has there been enough work for many of them to make a living, much less get rich. The men chosen for the chapters in this book are a very small number from a severely limited field, yet selected because their influence has been widespread and lasting. With the modern growth of the sport, more young designers have come into it and are making a name for themselves.

In a few years, some of them could very well rate inclusion in a list of "greats" and one or two are on the verge even now.

This is an American list, though of course there have been excellent men in other countries, notably Great Britain. The Americans in this book have been chosen because they have all gained more of an international reputation than yacht designers from other countries, and their designs have been seen and used in all parts of the world. You might say they have become household words, at least in yachting households.

There are foreign designers whose work has become known internationally. America's Cup competitions have spread the fame of such British designers as William Fife from the era of Sir Thomas Lipton's *Shamrocks,* and Charles Nicholson, whose two *Endeavours* of the 1930s have always been considered among the most beautiful of the J boats. More recently, Alan Payne and Warwick Hood of Australia have performed prodigies in turning out designs and supervising construction of America's Cup 12-Meter challengers from Australia. They did not meet with success; nonetheless, Payne's two *Gretels* in 1962 and 1970 were both conceded to be faster in many ways than the defenders, and *Gretel II* is thought by some to be the fastest 12-Meter developed up to that time. In the 1970s, Payne began designing directly for the American market with a line of stock auxiliaries.

In addition, Arthur Robb, Laurent Giles, John Illingworth, and Robert Clark are among the British designers whose work has become known internationally, and the German Frers, father and son, of Argentina have also been very successful. Scandinavian designers like Colin Archer, Johann Anker, Bjarne Aas, and Jan Linge have gained international recognition, as has E. G. van de Stadt from Holland.

But to return to America, and going back to the early days, there have been other yacht designers who experienced considerable success during their lifetimes, but whose names have lived on largely through the way their work influenced the men included in this book. A. Cary Smith was one of the first naval architects to specialize in yacht design, and the 1881 America's Cup defender, *Mischief,* a beamy iron centerboarder, was his best-known boat. In the previous Cup defenses in 1871 and 1876, the boats had been typical adaptations of the pilot schooner type; but *Mischief* embodied special thinking and was a true racing yacht. In 1885, Edward Burgess of Boston designed *Puritan,* the successful defense candidate, and he dominated the America's Cup field until his death in 1891, leaving the way open for Nathanael Herreshoff. The Burgess name returned to the scene in the 1930s after Captain Nat had designed his last defender, when Edward's son, W. Starling, turned out the great J-boat defenders *Enterprise, Rainbow,* and *Ranger.* The last was designed in collaboration with young Olin Stephens, who is still a vital part of the America's Cup picture in the 1970s. The line of descent in this competition has been indeed a long, thin, and sparsely populated one.

Among other successful designers of the great yachts in the years surrounding World War I, and on into the Depression era, was William Gardner, especially noted for the schooner *Atlantic,* holder of the record sail crossing of her namesake ocean, and the lovely Cup defense candidate *Vanitie.* Beautiful as she was, and as fast as she proved on many occasions, *Vanitie* could never quite beat out Herreshoff's *Resolute* in Cup trials. Gardner's assistant, Francis Sweisguth, gained fame on his own as designer of the Star, one of the first and most durable of the one-design classes.

B. B. Crowninshield was one of the leading yacht designers of the early twentieth century, and it was in his Boston office that John Alden served his apprenticeship. Crowninshield had several near-misses with America's Cup candidates but dealt in all sizes of boats. Later, when Alden had his own office, some of his assistants went on to make names for themselves—men like Aage Nielsen, Winthrop Warner, Carl Alberg, and Charles Wittholz.

Frank Paine was another successful New England designer, responsible for the J boat *Yankee,* and it was in his office that young Ray Hunt went to work. New England cruising yachtsmen were also very partial to the husky cruising boats of S. S. Crocker, and Nat Herreshoff's sons, A. Sidney deW. and L. Francis, carried on the family name, with the latter's *Ticonderoga* his top creation. Henry Gielow specialized in the largest luxury yachts until the Depression ended their era.

Bill Luders of Connecticut has long been noted for the originality of his thinking, as well as for his skill as a helmsman, though he often expressed a personal preference for tennis. Some of his suggestions helped turn *Weatherly* into the successful 1962 America's Cup defender. His own 12-Meter design, *American Eagle,* though beaten in the 1964 trials, went on to great success when converted to an ocean racer. Farther south, Fred Geiger of Philadelphia and Robert Henry of Oxford, Maryland, were noted for innovative auxiliary designs, Geiger with centerboarders ahead of the trend in the late fifties, and Henry with the 30-foot International 400, an able-racer cruiser that was a pacesetter in this type.

In the boom of the sixties and seventies, the profession gathered more new recruits. From such rising younger lights as George Cuthbertson and George Cassian (Canadians who operate as partners), Alan Gurney, Gary Mull, Charles Morgan, Bruce King, Halsey Herreshoff, and Britton Chance may come the greats of the next few years. All have had success with at least one boat, and in some cases with a large and varied body of work. C&C, as Cuthbertson and Cassian are familiarly called, have had such winners as the 1968 Southern Ocean Racing Conference (SORC) champ, *Red Jacket,* and a highly successful line of stock boats in many sizes. Gurney, a transplanted Englishman, has the big, record-holding ketch *Windward Passage* as his best-known product in an output that also includes stock boats. Gary Mull's 43-foot *Improbable* set an unheard-of record in winning the 871-mile Jamaica Race in 1971 at an average speed of 8.8 knots, and his stock boats have had great success. Bruce King's stock boats have moved into the top ranks, especially in West Coast competition, and Britton Chance has shown some truly innovative thinking in such boats as *Equation.* He was responsible for re-designing *Intrepid* for the 1970 America's Cup defense and was given a commission for a design of his own for 1974. He also turned out the French "trial horse" 12-Meter, *Chancegger.*

Charley Morgan became best known for his abortive one-man foray into America's Cup competition when he designed, built, made some sails for, was skipper of, and paid the bills for *Heritage* in the 1970 trials. He first gained special attention when his design *Paper Tiger* cleaned up in the 1961 SORC. She also pointed the way to the fiberglass revolution soon to hit the sport. Halsey Herreshoff, third generation in his family, has turned out successful boats that are highly reminiscent of his grandfather's.

In the cruising boat field, Frank MacLear, Spaulding Dunbar, and William Garden are among those who have turned out distinctive craft, and the powerboat category has produced Edwin Monk, Arthur DeFever, Blaine Seely, and John Hargraves as specialists in a thinly populated segment of the whole thinly populated profession.

As yachting continues to gain participants and to grow at every level, the lonely profession may gain more members. The art of designing a boat has such infinite variables, and has been studied and thought about by so relatively few men over the years, that the possibilities are there for all manner of change. If yacht designing had been subjected to the intense development and massive concentration of brains and manpower that have gone into the auto industry, the space program, the electronics field, or even breakfast foods, there is no telling what might have already come to pass.

An important advance in the profession, one that accelerated the pace of development after the 1930s, was the establishment of a towing tank for testing sailboat models in actual sailing aspects. The study took place at the Stevens Institute of Technology in Hoboken, New Jersey, and was pioneered by Professor

Kenneth Davidson, for whom it is now named. Starling Burgess and Olin Stephens made use of it for the 1937 America's Cup series in working on *Ranger,* the first Cup yacht to be tested in this way, although hulls had been tried in straight towing runs before. It is interesting that the Stevens tank is located near the Hudson River and the spot where over 100 years before Commodore John Cox Stevens, whose family gave the college its name, used to test-sail the models he carved himself before turning them over to a builder.

Ranger completely outclassed any previous J boats, easily defeating Charles Nicholson's *Endeavour II* and her American rivals for the defense berth. The second *Endeavour* was faster than the first one, which had been generally acknowledged as the fastest J boat up to that time, and the value of this special tank testing had been thereby dramatically demonstrated. A few other tanks have been established since then, and scientific studies have been undertaken on a small scale, but the profession is still far removed from the stage where the computer can take over. A boat's worth is still settled afloat and at sea, not in the towing tank, and the business of applying test data to the other elements that go into yacht design is still an intuitive art.

These other elements can be many and varied. A yacht designer is naturally subject, more than many other designers, to economic ups and downs, and he must also deal with strong-minded, individualistic clients. Often the design of a boat is the result of a real contest of wills between designer and owner, and, of course, many of the owners are wealthy men who have always had their way in business and private life. A designer must know how to deal with boatyards, and he must be up on such technical details as the strengths of materials and the latest in electronic equipment.

In addition, those who design for the ocean-racing set must also live constantly with "the rule." This broad term covers whatever measurement formula is currently in use for handicapping purposes, and the only thing certain about it is that it never remains the same for long. Designers are always talking about "the rule," a practice dating from the mid nineteenth century, when the formula took into account only waterline length and sail area. Since those early days, when it soon became apparent that any rule as simple as this could easily be beaten by a smart designer, rating rules have progressed through all sorts of stages. There have been various international and national systems, and one of the first in wide use was the Universal Rule in the early twentieth century.

As ocean racing grew more popular, and day racing fell more and more into the system of one-design classes racing boat-for-boat without handicaps, the major rules became mainly concerned with ocean racing. In the United States, the Bermuda Race Rule gradually evolved into the Cruising Club of America (CCA) Rule, administered by the club that sponsors the Bermuda Race, while in England the Royal Ocean Racing Club (RORC) Rule was in effect. Both of these rules went through many modifications and developments as fashions in ocean racers changed, and as one type or another "beat the rule" and had to be legislated against to keep racing equalized.

With ocean racing spreading internationally in the 1960s, and more and more boats crossing oceans to compete with other countries, the need for a single rule grew increasingly apparent. Through cooperation between the CCA and RORC and the International Yacht Racing Union, the single rule became a reality in the early 1970s and is known as the International Offshore Rule (IOR). It immediately went through several adaptations, or "Marks," and will no doubt continue to undergo sea change over the years. From a simple one-line formula concerning waterline length and sail area, a rule such as the IOR now requires a pamphlet of thirty pages or more, and designers can still find loopholes in it. As part of their profession, yacht designers will always be living with some form of "the rule."

Over the roughly 100 years in which yacht designing could be classed as a profession, just a few men, feeling their way on their own, with a relatively small body of work as precedent, have had that extra spark, that touch of intuition, that has resulted in accomplishments of a special mark. Their influence has been wide and lasting, and their stories follow.

Captain Nat (in straw hat)
at the yard in Bristol

Two

Nathanael Herreshoff

Of all the men who have worked in the field of yacht design, Nathanael Greene Herreshoff has had the widest and most lasting influence. Whole books have been written about his remarkable career, and condensing the scope of his achievement and influence into one chapter is not really doing him justice. The "Wizard of Bristol" belongs at the head of the list, chronologically and in stature.

The "Bristol" above is the old New England seaport town of Bristol, Rhode Island, on Narragansett Bay, and Herreshoff lived there for almost all of his ninety years, 1848 to 1938. For close to seventy years, he also worked there as a naval architect, engineer, inventor, and finally partner in the Herreshoff Manufacturing Company. His domination of the field of yacht design was so complete during the years 1890–1920 that they have often been referred to as "the Herreshoff era."

The Herreshoff tradition is still strong, though his last Cup defender sailed in 1920 and the last boat from his designs, the 52-foot yawl *Belisarius*, was launched in 1935. Two of his sons, L. Francis, who died in December 1972 at the age of eighty-two, and A. Sidney deW., carried on as yacht designers. Francis, who wrote the definitive biography of his father in 1953, lived in Marblehead, Massachusetts, in a unique stone building called "The Castle." He was best known for the 72-foot *Ticonderoga*, a graceful clipper-bowed ketch that at one time held most of the major course records in ocean racing. Sidney remained in Bristol and has been custodian of the family archives and memorabilia in a small museum in the family house hard by the former site of the Herreshoff yard. Sidney's son Halsey, an active naval architect and top competitive sailor, is known for designs strongly reminiscent of his grandfather's, especially in the distinctive "Herreshoff bow"—an almost straight overhang under pronounced sheer, with graceful hollowed sections. Halsey has also been partial to giving his boats such family names as *Alerion* and *Cosette.*

The generations have also carried on the family's physical traits. Herreshoff men are tall, lean, and wiry, laconic and shy until brought out, and speak with a distinct Rhode Island–brand New England twang.

Physical evidences of Captain Nat's influence are still at hand. *Belisarius* was still sailing in the 1970s, and perhaps the best-known modern reminder of the Herreshoff era is the 35-foot sloop *Dolphin* owned by the Lockwood family of New Suffolk, Long Island. Known as a Newport 29 (most Herreshoff boats were regularly referred to by their waterline length, considered the craft's most meaningful dimension), *Dolphin* was built in 1914 and remained one of the most successful racing auxiliaries on the Atlantic Coast right into the 1970s. Year after year, against waves of new boats representing the latest thinking and under many changes of measurement rules, *Dolphin* more than held her own. Her short ends and hollow bows are truly a Herreshoff trademark and they have shown modern sailors what the Wizard of Bristol produced, though many of them saw more of her stern than her bow.

There are still boats around from the classes known as NYYC 40s and 50s that raced for years on a one-design basis and were also converted into successful ocean racers, such as *Memory,* winner of the Bermuda Race in 1924, and *Rugosa II,* which took it in 1928. A Herreshoff boat with an especially interesting career is the Greek-owned *Alexandra Lisa,* the 103-foot yawl built from Captain Nat's 1928 designs as *Thistle.* Her unusual construction was five-sixteenths riveted bronze plates over steel frames, and she has worn her years well. After racing for years in top American events, she was sold to a Turkish owner and then to a Greek owner. She has survived stranding, years of neglect, and all manner of hard use.

Generations of New England youngsters have learned to sail in a class of small one-designs known variously at local clubs as Bullseyes and Herreshoff Twelves. Some are still actively racing, notably at Beverly Yacht Club, Marion, Massachusetts, and there has been a modern fiberglass adaptation. The S Class sloops on Long Island Sound and Narragansett Bay continue to provide top-notch one-design racing for an ardent group of loyalists. The 28-footers were first turned out in

His early work was on launches such as Scout.

Niagara III, *an 81-foot fast Herreshoff powerboat*
built for Howard Gould in 1901

1919 and sold for just under $2000. Over 150 were built and many are still in full racing condition. Their popularity came partly from the dividend that they could be used as overnighters and for limited cruising while providing one-design competition.

These are but a few continuing manifestations of the all-pervading influence that Captain Nat had in his prime, but it was actually the America's Cup that brought him his greatest fame. As has always been the case in this storied series, success in it has brought attention and renown beyond the world of yachting. The six defenses of the Cup between 1893 and 1920 were all by Herreshoff-designed boats—*Vigilant, Defender, Columbia* (twice), *Reliance,* and *Resolute*—all built by the company at Bristol. This dominance, along with the triumphs of so many other Herreshoff yachts, made Bristol practically the center of the yachting world for this era.

Conventional success with sailing yachts in the conventional tradition (though many of them were startling innovations in design when they came out) was only a part of the diverse story of Herreshoff's accomplishments and influence. He had a way with power yachts too and made his earliest reputation in that field. In an age in which millionaires vied to have the swiftest yachts possible, Herreshoff creations such as *Stiletto* showed the way, using experience gained in designing and building naval torpedo boats. Designing the engine as well as the hull was no problem for Nat, trained in engineering at the Massachusetts Institute of Technology, and this 94-foot craft with a beam of only 11½ feet could cruise easily at 20 knots, once made an eight-hour run at 26½ knots, and reached her greatest fame June 10, 1885, in a much-publicized race with the steamer *Mary Powell.* This Hudson River steamboat was considered the fastest vessel in the world at the time, and had beaten back many a challenge from other steamers. She was supposed to be capable of about 25 knots.

Stiletto, which the Herreshoff brothers had built for themselves in 1885, ranged alongside the *Powell* in a run on the Hudson, with Captain Nat in command in the pilothouse and many members of the press observing. For a while the long, slender *Stiletto* held even with the headlong rush of the big steamer, and then Captain Nat, deciding that everything was going well, jingled for added speed. *Stiletto* shot ahead, crossed the *Mary's* bow, dropped back and crossed her stern, then ranged ahead again, and after about thirty miles had a five-minute lead.

Stiletto's engine was an unusual one, and a step forward. In the power-yacht field she was considered a major breakthrough. Valves that let a heavy flow of steam in and out of the cylinders at top and bottom were an innovation with her, and her boiler was a development on the still new coil boiler invented by Nat's brother twelve years before.

From Nat's designs the Herreshoff company built the first torpedo boats for the U.S., British, French, Russian, and some South American navies, and his developments in boiler design and in steam engine improvements were as far-reaching in this field as his influence on sail.

In developing these boats for high-speed operation, Captain Nat also worked out wooden construction methods that were completely new at the time and have been standard ever since. He introduced screw fastenings for planking, and, by the strength of this method and the placing and stressing of smaller frames, he was able to save considerable weight over the ponderous traditional methods that depended on a mass of material.

A detailed study of his various inventions and innovations would turn up quite a list of Herreshoff "firsts" that have since become standard practice. He was responsible for such developments as hollow steel spars, crosscut sails, flat sterns on launches and steam yachts to prevent them from "squatting" at high speeds—forerunners of today's planing boats—and many refinements in rigging and fittings. Today they are taken for granted; when he did them, they were ingenious.

In the 1880s the Herreshoff company concentrated almost entirely on building steam yachts, except for some small racing catboats. Nat and his brother John Brown had formed a partnership to run the Herreshoff Manufacturing Company in 1878, and business was booming with the demand for steam yachts and torpedo boats. Many of them were big, comfortable yachts for cruising and living aboard, but the demand for speed was also met by such "launches" as the 98-foot *Javelin* for Edward D. Morgan and *Vamoose* for William Randolph Hearst.

Sailing was always Captain Nat's first love, however, and he had been active as a sailor all his life. He was a highly successful racing skipper from early youth on, and in the 1890s he went back to designing sailboats, all built by the company, while continuing his work with steam yachts and steam engines. His first sailboat design, the 25-foot *Violet,* was produced when he was sixteen and had a successful racing career of fifty years, and he turned out many small boats over the years since then. In Bristol he kept a small open sailboat ready for day sailing at any time of year that the weather was pleasant on Narragansett Bay. Moreover, when he traveled to places like the French Riviera, or in later years to a winter cottage in Coconut Grove, Florida, he always had a small boat to use, which he designed and then had built locally.

In the 1870s and 1880s, Captain Nat had experimented with catamarans, obtaining results that shook the sailing establishment to its foundations. Starting

Below, launching of Defender, *June 29, 1895, from the main shed at Bristol*

Right, the Herreshoff family escorting Mrs. Herreshoff Sr. to the launching

Above, Defender *jammed on the ways,
and tugs had to pull her off.*

*Handling Defender's enormous main.
Captain Nat is in dark suit
and fedora hat amidships.*

in 1875 with *Amarylis*, a 25-footer, he turned out a number of catamarans, including *John Gilpin Teaser, Tarantula, Goody-Two Shoes,* and *Lodola.*

According to tales and drawings brought back by whalers and voyagers, Polynesian natives were known to use two-hulled sailing vessels, but such crafts were not considered "civilized." Herreshoff had pondered this type of boat as a young man while sailing small catboats and sloops, and, as a form of leisure while working as a draftsman for the Corliss Steam Engine Company (a job he held before forming the partnership in the family firm), he turned out some designs and built them.

After experimenting with a lateen rig, he switched to a more conventional main and jib for better structural strength and sail control and took the catamaran *Amarylis* to the Open Centennial Regatta on Long Island Sound in June 1876. The major competition came from a few sandbaggers noted for their tough crews, and the Herreshoff craft took a razzing in the early stages of the race when the wind was light and the greater wetted surface of her two hulls held her back. When it came on to blow, however, *Amarylis* picked up and scooted by the whole fleet for an easy victory and the last laugh.

Captain Nat refined the type in several more boats, but eventually could find no competition and gave up the experimentation. Regatta officials reacted to the threat of these strange vessels by banning them from formal competition.

Turning from catamarans back to monohulls in the early 1890s, Captain Nat still managed to shake up the establishment with a series of innovations that had far-reaching effects. Popular at the time was a class of 46-footers, and Edward Morgan of the New York financial family, who had had the steam launch *Javelin* built by Herreshoff, wanted to get into it. In 1891 he acquired *Gloriana*, a Herreshoff-designed boat started for another owner who had to cancel, and that overworked word "breakthrough" could certainly be said to apply to this cutter.

The fashion of the day was a deep, sharp forefoot and relatively short overhangs, but Captain Nat designed *Gloriana* with a cutaway forefoot and what later became known as that "Herreshoff bow" of hollowed sections. Despite the overhanging ends, their longer diagonals gave her better sailing lines, the length of which were not taxed under the rule then in use. She was therefore allowed more sail area, and the buoyancy of the full ends gave her the stability to carry it effectively.

Gloriana made a shambles of the competition in her first year and created a rush of imitations, a psychology that no doubt still seems familiar to today's racing sailors. She accommodated to the water in an easy flowing way in contrast to the awkward pitching of her competitors, and she was also well ahead of her

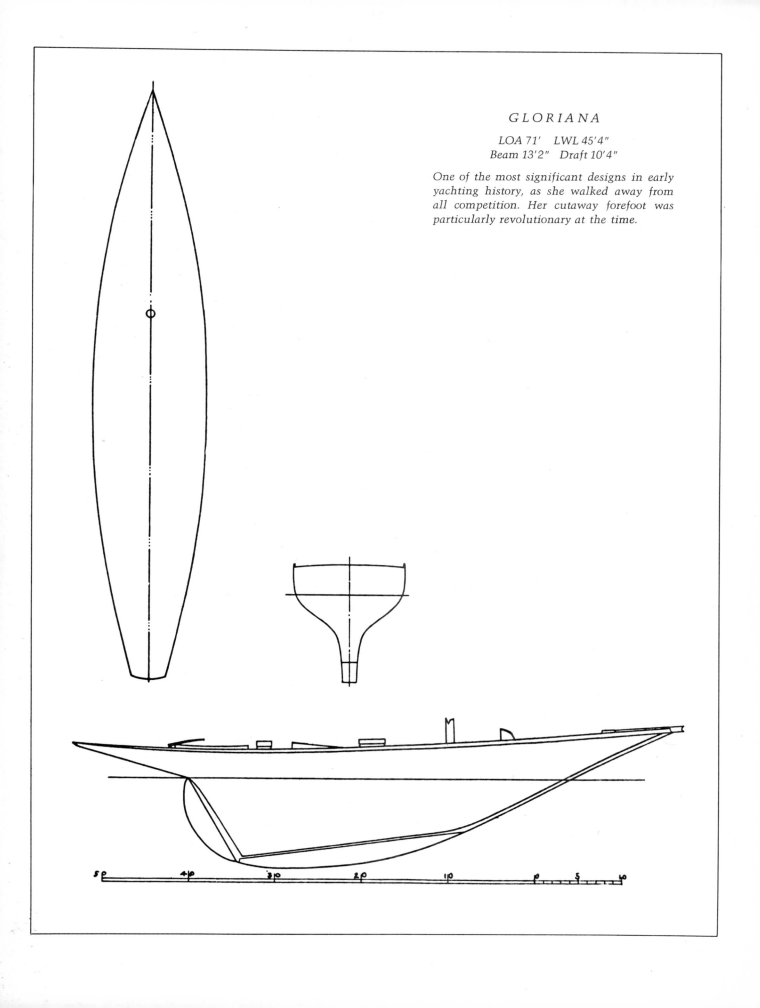

GLORIANA

LOA 71'   LWL 45'4"
Beam 13'2"   Draft 10'4"

One of the most significant designs in early yachting history, as she walked away from all competition. Her cutaway forefoot was particularly revolutionary at the time.

time in construction methods, fittings, and weight-saving. The Herreshoffs made all their own hardware and fittings, and these were employed in the boat's screw-fastened double planking over steel frames and strap diagonal framing. This double-planking method had been used in the fast launches, and differed from the nail-fastened single planing over sawn frames in general use on *Gloriana's* competitors. Her hatches, companionways, and deck fittings were kept extremely light so that all additional weight saved in that manner could be added to her ballast. She had special sail tracks (Nat was the inventor of the type of sail slides in use today), winches, turnbuckles, goosenecks, and many other fittings to go with her advanced hull design. With Morgan sailing the first race and Captain Nat at the helm for seven more, she won every race she entered, and then Morgan withdrew her to save the class. She remained a successful yacht for many years and a landmark in the development of racing sailboat design.

The same year, Herreshoff went even further with design innovations under sail by designing and building the first fin-keel racing boat, *Dilemma,* and he combined features of *Gloriana* and *Dilemma* in *Wasp,* another 46-footer, in 1892. She included *Gloriana's* above-water characteristics with a bulb fin keel. She was the first of many Herreshoff boats raced by a then-young professional skipper named Charles Barr, who eventually became the greatest racing skipper of his day. The fin-keelers had separate balanced rudders aft, which might surprise some who thought this was a modern development.

The success of these boats, and the death in 1891 of Edward Burgess, who had designed the three previous America's Cup defenders, opened the way for Herreshoff's selection as designer of *Vigilant* for the 1893 series. His dominance of the field began with this commission and lasted until 1920.

The Burgess and Herreshoff families were distantly related and had kept up a friendship for many years. Edward Burgess and Nat were the same age and were in college in Boston (Burgess at Harvard, Nat at M.I.T.) at the same time. The Burgess family, wealthy from shipowning and sugar plantations in Cuba, owned several Herreshoff yachts, and Edward Burgess often came to Bristol. He rose to the top of his profession quickly and at an early age, while Captain Nat was more involved with steam engines and launches. His untimely death, coinciding with Herreshoff's astounding success with *Gloriana,* opened the way for the Herreshoff string of six Cup defenders and allowed Herreshoff to become a nationally known figure.

In view of this great success, what was the background of this man, whose body of work was so varied and influential that even a seventy-year career seems

Vigilant *was a lovely example of Herreshoff's work,*
and his first defender. She was a deep centerboarder,
124 feet o.a., and constructed in 1893,
the first large yacht ever built of Tobin bronze.

Left, Columbia, *two-time defender of the America's Cup*

Measuring a defender was a serious—and well-dressed—job.
Above, Columbia *being measured in Brooklyn*

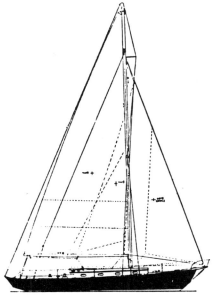

ROGUE

LOA 36'9"   LWL 29'
Beam 10'6"   Draft 5'4"
SA 800

The Herreshoff New Bedford 29, a 1914 design that remained competitive for 60 years, showed the strong sheer and hollowed bow sections that were Herreshoff trademarks.

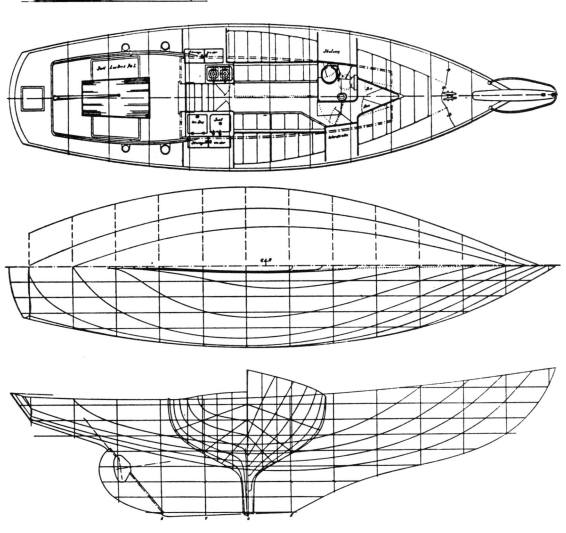

too short to have allowed time for everything? The Herreshoff family, which seems to be the only one in the United States by that name, is descended from a German student, an orphan who came to New York in 1787 to enter the importing business and anglicized his name from Carl Friederich Herrschhoff to Charles Frederick Herreshoff. In 1798 he had some business with John Brown, the Providence shipping merchant who compiled one of America's earliest fortunes, and ended up moving to Providence, living with the Browns, and eventually marrying their daughter Sarah. Herreshoff and his new wife settled at one of Brown's country estates—Point Pleasant Farm on Popasquash Neck, the western side of Bristol Harbor—and the family has been in the area ever since. Their son, also Carl Frederick, married Julia Lewis of Boston, a Mayflower descendant, and they raised nine children at Point Pleasant Farm. All of them lived to an advanced age, but four suffered from glaucoma and eventually lost their sight. The oldest boy, John Brown Herreshoff, always referred to as "J.B." by the family, went blind in his teens, while in the midst of building his first boat, *Meteor;* this misfortune had a profound effect on his brother Nat, seven years his junior, who remained keen-eyed throughout his life despite the long hours spent over tables of figures.

Instead of engaging in the usual childish pursuits, young Nat, at age nine, began acting as his brother's eyes. They sailed together in *Meteor* and in subsequent boats, and Nat also worked in the shop with J.B., guiding the older boy's hands over the machines and tools and in the process picking up much technical knowledge himself. Eventually they became business partners in the shipyard and found their talents complemented each other perfectly: J.B. had a fantastic faculty for figuring costs and working out production details, and Nat was doing drafting work in his early teens.

Nat, who was named for the Revolutionary general Nathanael Greene, a family friend of the Browns, was slender and wiry and remained healthy except for rheumatism. His personality was taciturn, forthright, and blunt. He didn't waste words, and he was very sure of himself. Grandson Halsey tells a family story of Nat and one of his brothers standing on the pier one day. Nat said, "Umph," and the brother said, "Hmmph," and a sister, overhearing them, ran to their mother and said, "Come quickly. The boys are having a terrible argument."

He was a teetotaler, even to the extent of eschewing coffee, tea, or any other stimulant, but his son Francis reports in his biography that Captain Nat was persuaded to take a drink just once, when *Columbia* beat *Shamrock* resoundingly in a cold beat to windward in the America's Cup race on October 20, 1899. At the celebration afterward, Mrs. C. Oliver Iselin, wife of the owner, who had sailed aboard throughout the campaign, was the successful persuader.

The S Class sloop has had an enduring career.

His early interest in things scientific was put to good use at M.I.T., and while a freshman there in 1866, he spent the winter working out a table of allowances for handicap racing at the request of some men in the Boston Yacht Club that, with a few changes, remains the basis for the tables still in use today. After college, he spent some time traveling abroad and put in nine years in the draftsman's job for Corliss Steam Engine Company in Providence.

A remarkable feature of the trip abroad was that he and his blind brother Lewis built a 17-foot sloop, *Riviera,* with their own hands; they then cruised her along the Mediterranean coast, and, by sail and oars, through the rivers and canals of France and Holland. Following this, they took her on a steamer to England, cruised there for a while, and brought her home by steamer to New York. She was dropped into the harbor from the steamer's deck and they promptly set out under sail for Narragansett Bay. The hand-made boat remained in the family until the boathouse where she was stored was wrecked in the 1938 hurricane.

When Captain Nat returned to Bristol and became a partner with J.B., he settled into a routine that was to last for many years; he would work twelve hours a day, seven days a week, except on those Sundays when he tried to get some sailing in. He worked at home on the models from which he developed his designs, and at his drafting board, alternating early morning and evening hours there with supervisory visits to the yard during the working day. All of his boats were developed from models and there are no line drawings of the yachts and boats he designed. He would make a preliminary sketch and then develop the model from that, and the final operation of many careful steps was a meticulous sanding of the hull form to eliminate any imperfections or irregularities.

Although he used many drawings and calculations for construction plans, engine designs, rigging, and strength calculations, his development of hull forms was, as his son Francis put it, "pure art."

He remained a bachelor until he was thirty-five, when he married Clara DeWolf, the eldest daughter of some good friends of his parents who had a long background in shipping and seafaring. They had six children in nine years, and Francis remembers Nat as a kind father, who made sure his children had toys and boats to play with, but who did not have much time to spend with them in the rigors of his working schedule. He designed and had built a house on a promontory in the harbor known as Love Rocks, within quick walking distance of activities at the yard. It was there that the family grew up. In summer, Mrs. Herreshoff took the children to a farm belonging to her family a bit out in the country from Bristol, but Captain Nat spent very little time there, as it took him out of immediate touch with the yard and his models. Often, he slept alone in the Love

Rocks house, or even on one of the boats at the yard, so that he could be near the yard at all times.

Captain Nat seldom had any social engagements, and his life at home revolved around his work. Mrs. Herreshoff was an excellent cook, and he ate well with a good appetite, but the family did not see too much of him otherwise. For long hours in the early morning and then again in the evening, he was in his study.

The best-known result of all these labors was, of course, the string of Cup defenders. These boats were in action during an era when the America's Cup races were front-page news—far beyond the normal sports coverage—and the people involved naturally became public celebrities. No other sport, except possibly horse racing, received as much attention as sailing, and sailing was also the first international sport. Royalty was involved, led by the Prince of Wales, later Edward VII, and America's Cup principals like Lord Dunraven, Charlie Barr, Herreshoff, and Sir Thomas Lipton were as well known to the public as today's pro athletes, movie stars, and jet setters.

Despite the public attention and the chance to rub shoulders with other celebrities, Captain Nat maintained his concentration on the practical side of the preparations—the design of the boats and the engineering details. In 1894, he was asked to supervise operations in England with *Vigilant,* bought by George Gould for the purpose of campaigning there, and he was on the Gould steam yacht one day when the Prince of Wales came aboard and asked to meet *Vigilant's* designer. Seeing the group coming, Herreshoff hid in the engine room until they went away.

The 1895 defender, aptly named *Defender,* presented some peculiar problems. First of all, she refused to go down the ways at her launching. As cannon boomed and crowds cheered, she slid out of the shop doors "a moving dream of white and gold," as a contemporary account had it, but the cheering died to embarrassed murmurs when she came to a stop halfway down. Eventually it took a diver to remove an obstructing lag bolt from the ways before she belatedly hit the water. All this was very embarrassing to a Boston reporter who had tried to score a scoop by filing his story early, complete with flowing descriptions of the dramatic dash down the ways and how beautiful she looked riding in the water.

Also, Captain Nat had been sick when *Defender's* mast step was built, and it gave trouble before he was able to find that some rivets had been left out of a place that couldn't be inspected easily. This problem solved, she began to have trouble with the aluminum in her construction. Little was known about aluminum's properties, though its strength had been tested, and it began to deteriorate

Memory, *a New York 40, won the Bermuda Race in 1924.*

Reliance, *1903, was the largest defender ever, 90 feet on the water,
144 feet o.a., with 16,160 feet of sail. She had many radical advances
in design and equipment and initially cost $175,000,
exclusive of special equipment. She, too, was of Tobin bronze.*

Hundreds of junior sailors have trained in the Herreshoff Bullseye.

when in contact with bronze in a saltwater atmosphere. Despite these problems, however, she was fast, and her match against Lord Dunraven's *Valkyrie III* was the most controversial of any in Cup history. Amid fouls, accusations, and counterclaims, all aired in great detail in the press, Lord Dunraven was stripped of his honorary membership in the New York Yacht Club and went home mad. It wasn't until Sir Thomas Lipton appeared on the scene with the first of his five *Shamrock*s that an era of better feeling and sportsmanship began. Captain Nat was in the thick of it with *Columbia,* considered by many to be his best Cup yacht. With Barr as skipper, she twice defended the Cup, the only yacht to do so until *Intrepid,* 1967–70.

The 1903 yacht *Reliance* was the biggest, at 149 feet overall, ever to sail for the Cup, and she contained many of Captain Nat's special innovations. She was built from the first model he made, which took him about two days, an interesting contrast to the months of tank testing for the modern 12-Meter campaigns. She was 89 feet on the water, and her tremendous spread of 16,000 feet of sail gave her the maximum dimension of 201 feet from the end of her bowsprit to the end of her main boom.

Captain Nat designed many of her fittings and had them custom-made, doing his own testing of the strengths required, based on the vast amount of data he had accumulated about the strains that occur on a large racing sailboat. She had very light spars and nine of her winches were below deck, including two-speed self-releasing ones for wire sheets and backstays, using such items as worm gears, multiple-disk clutches and ball bearings—all relatively unknown at that time of auto industry infancy. Some of these same winches were used repeatedly on subsequent Cup yachts right up to *Ranger* in 1937.

Reliance had a lightweight rudder of thin bronze sheets over a frame that could be made heavier by pumping water in when more heft was needed for heavy going. She had two steering wheels for easier relieving under way, with foot-controlled brake pedals on them for added control of sensitivity. Of all Nat's boats, *Reliance* probably best exemplified his knowledge of building to the rule in effect and his engineering ingenuity. She was called the most scientifically designed sailing vessel ever built and still rates high on that list today.

It might be said that the Herreshoff "era" ended with *Resolute.* She was built for a 1914 series that was delayed by World War I until 1920, and she carried on many characteristics of a general era that had really ended in 1914. No longer was yachting carried on at the scale that had made the Herreshoff yard the virtual capital of the sport for so long; the principals in the firm were dead or had grown old. Captain Nat was over seventy when his last Cup yacht won her series, and,

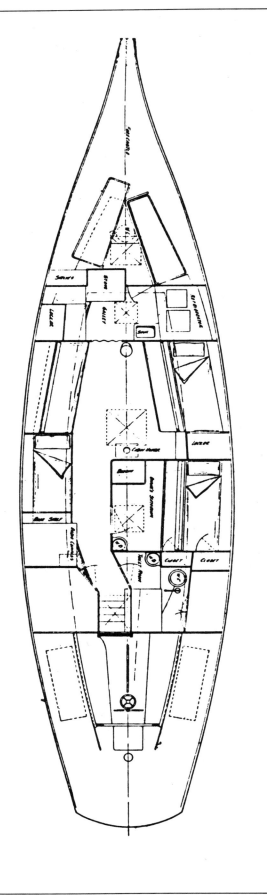

BELISARIUS

LOA 56'2"   LWL 41'
Beam 14'   Draft 5'8"
SA 1413

Captain Nat's last design included many of
his touches, especially in the sheer and bow,
with a rig that was thoroughly modern for
the time, 1935.

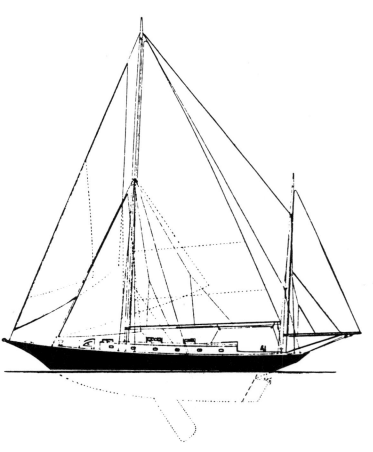

The graceful yawl Belisarius, *1935, was Herreshoff's last design.*

though his active era was about over, the body of his work would be long re-membered.

Today the sheds and buildings of the Herreshoff Manufacturing Company have mostly disappeared, and the Bristol waterfront is the quieter for it. There are modern marinas and moored yachts, and the Sidney Herreshoffs have pre-served Herreshoff memorabilia in the small museum in their waterfront home. A great deal of construction of fiberglass auxiliaries is carried on in the area at inland locations, but the great steam yachts and America's Cup defenders are gone. There are many old-timers who still remember them, however, and also recall the sight of the slender, slightly stooped, bearded figure making the rounds of the work projects in the yard, and then walking back in the calm of an evening, when the afternoon southwester that blows up Narragansett Bay almost every afternoon had faded to a whisper, to spend more time laboring on the models and the more than 18,000 drawings that were the working output of the uniquely influential Wizard of Bristol.

Dolphin, *designed in 1914, was still winning races in the 1970s.*

Clinton H. Crane

Three

Clinton H. Crane

The name Clinton H. Crane may not be on the lips of today's yachtsmen as often as Olin Stephens or Bill Lapworth, and the influence carried on from his work is not as widespread as that generated by the incredibly varied output of Nathanael Herreshoff, but the modern sailor still owes a debt in many ways to the designer, skipper, and racing official who died in 1958 at the age of eighty-five. His was a long and distinguished career that saw him involved in many phases of the sport.

His career was unusual in that it began with racing and amateur designing, and then saw Crane switch to a full-time professional for a dozen years, take up an entirely different business for over a decade, and then return to sailing as an amateur. In these later years, even as an amateur, he was one of the most important men in the field. His involvement with all types of yachting meant that from racing motorboat to ocean-going steam yacht, from light centerboarder to America's Cup J boat, his designs were influential and very successful in their amazing display of versatility.

One of his last design involvements was with the 12-Meter Class and its growth in the 1930s, and the success of Crane-designed boats and of Crane himself as a skipper had a great deal to do with establishing the current America's Cup class in this country. He had the 12-Meter *Gleam* built to his own designs in

1937 as his own racing yacht and campaigned her with considerable success when the fleet on Long Island Sound consisted of *Seven Seas* (also from his design), *Gleam, Nyala, Northern Light, Vim,* and some other boats. *Gleam,* converted to cruising, was active in New York Yacht Club racing until very recently.

Olin Stephens, in designing *Vim* for Harold S. Vanderbilt in 1938, was charged with outdesigning the Crane Twelves to give Vanderbilt a faster boat, and the line of descent to the modern Stephens Twelves was initiated.

The Crane career had its beginnings when he was still an undergraduate in Harvard. His first sailing had been in canoes at a summer camp in New Hampshire. His college-age sailing was first done in a scaled-down, deep narrow boat similar to British cutters, and then in a 13-foot centerboarder of his own design. The comparative success of the latter convinced him that a light boat, utilizing shifting crew weight for ballast, had a higher performance potential, and this had much to do with the development of his thinking and the type of boats he started designing.

After graduation from Harvard in 1894 his first job was as an apprentice machinist at Cramp's Shipyard, Philadelphia. His early ambition was to design ocean liners, but this changed when he became active in sailboat racing. A top trophy of the era was the Seawanhaka Cup for international competition and Crane decided to go into it in 1896 with *El Heirie,* a 15-footer of his own design. The rule for handicapping was the old Seawanhaka one of l.w.l. plus the square root of the s.a. divided by two. He had the boat built at the Lawley yard near Boston and delivered to the Sound. He and his brother Henry were unknown as racing sailors, and had, in fact, no formal racing experience when they sailed her from Rye, New York, over to the Seawanhaka Corinthian Yacht Club at Oyster Bay to join a crack fleet of twenty-eight boats, all under top skippers and from the boards of the best designers. The upstart newcomers won the opener and were eventually selected to defend the trophy, but the success story stopped there for the moment.

Their opponent was G. Herrick Duggan, an experienced Canadian skipper and designer of considerable fame, and they lost to him and the scow *Glencairn* in three straight races. The Crane boys continued to win the American eliminations for the next three years, but they couldn't catch up with Duggan's very advanced work with scow-type boats, and the Seawanhaka Cup remained north of the border. *Glencairn II* and then *Dominion,* a scow with a "tunnel" hull that made her almost a form of catamaran, were the Duggan creations that beat Crane's *Momo* and *Seawanhaka.* Moreover, when *Dominion*'s radical conformation was outlawed, Duggan went back to a conventional scow, *Glencairn III,* and defeated

The schooner Dervish *won the second Bermuda Race in 1907.*

Crane's *Constance.* (Much later, in 1925, Crane had the pleasure of winning the Cup in his 6-Meter, *Lanai.*)

These experiences had a strong influence on the development of the career of the young Crane, who was continuing his engineering studies at Columbia and then at Glasgow, and also had an effect on the establishment of the light-displacement, planing type of boat, as exemplified by the scows, on the North American racing scene. Crane felt he had learned much from Duggan about light-weight construction as well as design.

Deciding to go full time into yacht designing after completion of his studies in Scotland, where he had had a rare opportunity to get to know British yacht designers and to study their work, Crane accepted an offer to join the brokerage firm of Tams and Lemoine as its design partner. He also had offers to go with two of the best-known designers of the day, A. Cary Smith and William Gardner, but decided that he would rather be on his own than playing second fiddle to an established senior partner and the firm became Tams, Lemoine and Crane. He joined it in 1899 and went on the "masthead" in 1900.

This was the era of the great yachts, the magnificent luxury vessels of colorful memory, and also of the early growth of motorboating, and Crane became deeply involved in both. His first assignment in the speedboat field was from a firm that imported foreign automobiles and wanted to publicize their 24-horsepower Panhard engines. Crane was asked to design a boat that could use the engine, which also meant designing the propeller, as there were no stock ones available. The boat, *Vingt-et-un,* hit 22.5 m.p.h. and was considered a nautical and promotional success. In fact, the auto firm asked for a larger boat, *Vingt-et-un II,* with a 75-horsepower engine, and she was matched in a race against Nat Herreshoff's fast steam launch *Swift Sure.* Herreshoff was not convinced that the gasoline engine was here to stay and felt that a small steam engine could be as fast and much more reliable, but *Vingt-et-un II,* by beating *Swift Sure* handily in a race at Newport, Rhode Island, changed the mind of the Wizard of Bristol. He later built *XPDNC,* with a Mercedes gas engine, and she beat *Vingt-et-un II* in a race from New York to Poughkeepsie.

This powerboating success led to involvement in the Harmsworth Trophy, an international competition for speedboats. Crane's first candidate, *Challenger,* caught fire on a trial run in the Harlem River and the crew had to abandon ship and swim for it. There were four in crew and only three life jackets, so Crane, a strong swimmer, went without one, swimming with his pants and sweater held up in one hand. They made for a nearby ferry boat, and clambered aboard safely—

Dixie II, *after winning the 1909 Gold Cup at Alexandria Bay, N.Y.*

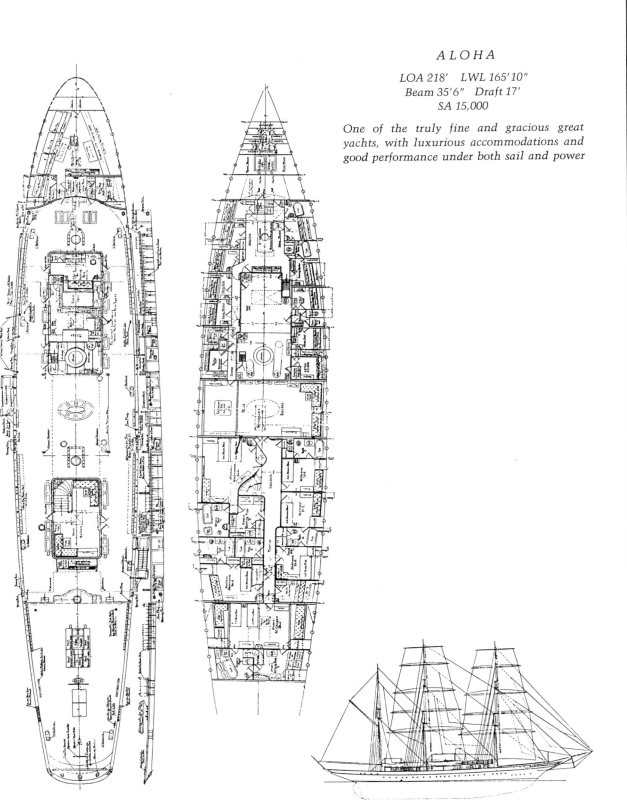

ALOHA

LOA 218'   LWL 165'10"
Beam 35'6"   Draft 17'
SA 15,000

*One of the truly fine and gracious great
yachts, with luxurious accommodations and
good performance under both sail and power*

to Crane's considerable embarrassment, since the vessel seemed loaded with women and he was stark naked.

Challenger failed in her quest for the Harmsworth in England when her engineer, against orders, took a spray hood off the engine and the wake of a passing steamer drowned it out. Eventually, Crane's *Dixie,* which exceeded her guaranteed speed of 30 m.p.h., won the Harmsworth, and *Dixie II,* which got up to 36 m.p.h., retained it. Crane pushed the speed up to 47 m.p.h. with *Dixie IV* but lost interest in high-speed powerboats when it became evident that hydroplanes, not displacement hulls, were the answer. *Dixie II* was the last displacement Harmsworth winner; Crane considered hydroplanes unsound and not a design challenge.

In sail, one of his first successful professional designs was the sloop *Lanai* in the raceabout class, a popular small-boat type that would be called a development class today. Using some of the construction techniques and ideas on hull form gained in the Seawanhaka Cup series, he made her very light, and she cleaned up in the class in Long Island Sound, Buzzards Bay, and Maine. She was so much faster than her competition that she was used in team races to drop back and blanket boats from the other team, thus letting her own team members through. They developed a technique, when a team member was close, of increasing the latter's speed on a reach by having *Lanai* "tow" the other boat on her quarterwave; something akin to wake surfing. *Lanai* had been built for Arthur Curtiss James, who then turned to the young designer for his next big yacht. This was *Aloha,* a 127-foot hermaphrodite brig, built in 1899, and Crane's first major yacht. He wanted to make her very fast, with a big rig and the ballast to carry it, but the owner's requirements for accommodations came first, and Crane had to alter plans: an early lesson in designer-client relationships. Since James also had Crane design the next *Aloha* in 1910, a 218-foot steel bark and one of the most beautiful yachts in history, his accommodation to the accommodations was not a mistake. *Aloha* made a leisurely, luxurious circumnavigation of the world soon after World War I on a voyage that was notable mainly for how smoothly everything went. In another bit of tactful client relations with the James family, Crane found just before the launching that the first *Aloha*'s figurehead, which was of Mrs. James, had been done as a nude by the sculptor and, at the last minute, James had it draped with some "robes."

Soon after the first *Aloha,* he designed the big schooner *Endymion,* whose owner wanted to set speed records, including one to Bermuda. Crane advised that the way to accomplish this was to wait until a winter northwester was about to set in, so *Endymion* was taken to Sandy Hook, New Jersey, in early February 1900 and was all ready to go when the proper prediction came through. Off she went in a smother of foam under four lowers. It breezed on to a full gale, and they shortened to a squaresail, staysail, and jib; but the squaresail blew right out of its boltropes, flying on over the bow in the clear, starry night, and for two days she surged on under bare poles. Though seasick, Crane crawled aft to the stern to watch the action of the big waves coming up under the long counter stern. He had been advised against a long overhang but had used one anyway and was pleased to see that it rose well to the onrushing combers. With a cutaway forefoot, long keel, and rudder well aft, *Endymion* steered well, but he did learn that closed bulwarks held too much water on deck for too long as *Endymion* rolled in the heavy seas. She ran into a calm off Bermuda and lost any chance for the record, arriving in eighty hours (the current Bermuda Race record is seventy hours set by *Bolero* in 1956) and everyone aboard had had a miserable time with seasickness. In June, *Endymion* cleared Sandy Hook in a fresh southwester that she carried for four days, then picked up a northwester that held all the way to England, and set the transatlantic sailing-ship record of thirteen days, eight hours, Sandy Hook to the Needles, that held for five years until broken by *Atlantic* in the 1905 Transatlantic Race.

Another Crane schooner, Henry T. Morss's *Dervish,* won the 1907 Bermuda Race, and all these racing yachts added to his reputation, but the way to make money in the yacht business in the first decade of the twentieth century was in the mammoth steam luxury yachts, and the firm of Tams, Lemoine and Crane was well involved. The largest and best known of many turned out by the firm was C. G. K. Billings' 277-foot *Vanadis. Vanadis* was built in Scotland, and, through a miscalculation, not enough coal was put aboard for her delivery voyage to the U.S. in 1908. Before she arrived, much of the handsome paneling in her salons and staterooms had been stripped away and fed to the stokehold fires to keep her going. Special features of *Vanadis* included a carbonic acid gas refrigerator that could make 500 pounds of ice per day, and special chocks on her foredeck for carrying a big touring car.

Crane had some interesting encounters with his wealthy clients, including a wild auto ride through Brooklyn with W. K. Vanderbilt, who was very fond of fast cars. Henry Clay Pierce, the oil millionaire who was the one told by J. P. Morgan that "if you ask how much it would cost to run a yacht you have no right to own one," was a difficult client who didn't worry about costs when ordering items but screamed bloody murder when the bills came in. Crane's firm was consulting for him on the conversion of a British yacht he had bought, for which he had ordered all sorts of special work. She had a large refrigerator, enormous grocery

The beautiful bark Aloha, in which Arthur Curtiss James made a circumnavigation

Crane's J boat design Weetamoe
almost made it to the defender's berth in 1930.

bins, custom interior decoration with silk panels, gold-plated hardware, and gold fittings in the bathrooms. Scenting trouble, Crane had every order written down and approved by Pierce as it was given. When the inevitable reckoning came and Pierce balked, putting the bills in the hands of a lawyer, the written confirmations saved the day. Joseph Pulitzer, the publisher, tried to get Crane to "guarantee" that the operating expenses for Vanderbilt's *Valiant,* which he was considering buying, would not exceed $150,000—much to Crane's amusement, as he himself had no personal fortune.

At the peak of this career, in 1912, he was forced to leave yacht designing and step into the management of St. Joseph Lead Company, which his father had founded and which was in shaky condition. Within a year he was president, and the firm was back in healthy shape. He remained with it until he retired, as president until 1947, and then chairman of the board, but, as successful as he was as a mining engineer, his first love was still yachting. He maintained his membership in many clubs and became active in the North American Yacht Racing Union, of which he was made president in 1949, and also continued as a racing skipper. In the 1920s, with less responsibility in the Lead Company, which was running well, he took up yacht designing on an amateur basis and achieved his most important design, the J boat *Weetamoe.* He had been working with 6- and 8-Meters through the twenties with considerable success, and it was felt that his design genius should be used in the revival of the America's Cup, after a ten-year lapse, in 1930.

At first there was talk of cooperative design work among Starling Burgess, L. Francis Herreshoff, Frank Paine, and Crane, but the eventual decision was to have them all work separately. The results were *Enterprise, Whirlwind, Yankee,* and *Weetamoe,* respectively. Crane had no real office and therefore moved into the drafting room of the big firm of Cox and Stevens to work on *Weetamoe's* plan. George Nichols was syndicate head and skipper, and the boat was built at the Herreshoff yard in Bristol, Rhode Island, where Crane was delighted to have the advantage of much of the special gear and equipment developed by Captain Nat Herreshoff for earlier Cup boats.

In retrospect, in his book, *Clinton Crane's Yachting Memories,* published in 1952, Crane expressed the opinion that he, and all the other designers but Francis Herreshoff, made a mistake in not going to the top limits allowed in the J Class rule; nonetheless, *Weetamoe* was bigger than *Enterprise* and seemed to be clearly the leading candidate in the early trials. *Yankee* didn't go well in light air, *Whirlwind* was powerful but never seemed properly tuned, and *Enterprise* seemed slightly less of an all-round boat than *Weetamoe.* However, Harold Vanderbilt and his team on *Enterprise* kept working all summer at improving her rig, installing a

lighter mast and making ballast adjustments. On the theory that you don't tamper with a winner, *Weetamoe* did not use the lighter mast she had in storage, and other adjustments Crane had contemplated were not tried. Then, when *Enterprise* began to put it all together, it was too late to make changes in *Weetamoe*. With Vanderbilt having the better of tactics in some key situations, *Enterprise* came on with a late rush to get the defender's assignment. *Weetamoe,* however, had left behind the impression that she had a great potential. By 1934, she had been somewhat outbuilt but still was in the thick of that year's trials until near the end.

Although *Weetamoe* was the peak of this "amateur" career, the 12-Meter accomplishments that followed were a fitting finale and an important bridge, in one designer's lifetime, from the late nineteenth century to the very modern world of the new Twelves. Few careers have been more versatile or more successful than Clinton Crane's.

Crane's own 12-Meter Gleam *had a great influence on the modern generation of Twelves.*

John Alden where he loved to be,
at the wheel of a boat at sea

Four

John Alden

Before World War I, the average yachtsman did not go offshore very much, and coastal cruising was also a very limited activity. There were the venturesome singlehanders like Slocum, Voss, and their imitators; rich men put professionally manned luxury yachts into an occasional Transatlantic Race; and the Bermuda Race had been started but faltered and faded—but it was rare for an owner to range very far in his own boat. Most of the yachting activity was in day-sailing races in light, shallow "skimming dishes" around the buoys in protected water, although some of the "day-sailers" were mammoth racing machines. Large cruises were very unusual ventures.

Comparing a general situation of this sort to the vast amount of offshore racing, cruising, and passaging that takes place today indicates that a great change has taken place, and one man was the single most important catalyst in bringing this change about. John Alden was the yacht designer (and sailor) who had the most to do, especially in the twenties and thirties, with bringing yachtsmen and offshore work together; his influence was profound too on the gentler art of coastal cruising, which also grew by tremendous leaps during those decades. Yet things have moved so fast in the world of racing and cruising auxiliaries that there are no doubt many active participants in the sport today who are not fully aware of

White Wing *celebrated her fiftieth anniversary in 1974*
and is a typical example of the popular stock Alden 43-foot schooner.

what the name John Alden meant to the development of it only a few years ago. He died in 1962.

In this age of low wetted surface, short keels, spade rudders, trim tabs, Dacron, nylon, aluminum, fiberglass and rod rigging, the world of John Alden's husky adaptations of commercial fishing types seems much more remotely past than it actually is. He was thoroughly capable of keeping up with the times himself, and through the thirties and forties his ocean-racing designs continued to be successful, owing a debt to the old fisherman type but advancing and developing on it. All of his designs were so basically able and sound that his boats had a long life in both racing and cruising; many of them can be seen in cruising harbors today, though not so many are actively racing. He put seaworthiness and soundness first before worrying about a boat's rating; but this didn't mean that his boats were slow.

John himself was a complete sailor and yachtsman, not just a genius of the drawing board. He looked and acted like a seaman and was never happier than when he was offshore in one of his own creations, getting every inch out of her through his fantastic touch with sail trim and at the helm. A husky man of medium size, with a close-cropped head of white hair in his later years, he had the ruddy complexion and steady eye of a deep-sea sailor and a voice that could carry through the whine of wind in a schooner's multitudinous "strings" or tell a recalcitrant customer in no uncertain terms just what was wrong with some ideas proposed for a new boat. He was laconic in the best New England tradition, with an economy of phrasing that got to the point quickly, and he never stood on ceremony very much.

I recall returning from the SORC in the late 1950s on a plane loaded with men who had been racing, most of them duded out in city clothes or yachting blazers; but John Alden, carrying an old seabag, was comfortable in a faded denim shirt, khaki pants, and Top Siders and not worried about the incongruity of his costume in the fancy airport surroundings.

Although his name and manner were New England to the core, and his nickname was "John o' Boston" to yachtsmen, he was actually born in Troy, New York, at the headwaters of navigation for the Hudson River. The family roots were deep in New England, however, and from his earliest years he summered at Little Compton, Rhode Island, on Sakonnet Point at the western end of Buzzards Bay. Here, in the fresh southwesterlies the area is famous for, he first learned to sail. At age six he was punished for taking his older sister's rowboat out on a pond without permission, and by age ten he was racing a little catboat in a junior fleet on salt ponds inside the beach.

Left, Teragram *was one of the better-known Alden schooners.*

*Below, the O Class sloop was an example
of a smaller Alden one-design.*

Tiring of the limited pond sailing, the youngsters lugged the boats across the barrier beach one day and raced around an offshore island. It was after dark before they returned home to worried parents, but from then on pond sailing was out.

In 1901, when John was sixteen, Sakonnet Yacht Club replaced the catboats with a new class of open 21-foot knockabouts. The young lad, conceiving a scheme that was typical of his personality and his approach to sailing, had the new boat delivered to Troy so that he could sail her to Sakonnet himself. He started with another boy as a companion, but became a singlehander when the crew jumped ship after the boat was strained going through some rapids, requiring constant pumping, and then capsized at anchor in a squall in Haverstraw Bay. A tug rescued the crew, who kept on going home, but John righted his boat and continued his passage via the Hudson and Harlem rivers and Long Island and Block Island sounds.

He managed to negotiate the tricky waters of the Harlem and East rivers by himself, but by the time he got into Long Island Sound, well behind schedule, he was broke and just about out of food. Canned franks, tomato sauce, and bread were the only supplies left when he tied up to the bulkhead of a Connecticut estate for the night. The butler came down to chase him away but became so impressed with the young sailor's plight that he took him back to the house instead and gave him a square meal and a dry bed in the staff quarters on the understanding the boat would clear the bulkhead before the estate owner, John Sherman Hoyt, came down at 6:30 for his morning swim.

It was raining and blowing hard out of the east the next day, and John hadn't gotten away when Mr. Hoyt, despite the weather, came down to the shore. When he heard John's story, he told him it was no day to set out to the eastward and invited him up to the house for breakfast, this time in the dining room, with his friend of the night before serving him. Even then, young John wanted to be a yacht designer, and he happened to mention his ambition to Mr. Hoyt. And in storybook fashion, twenty-five years later, Hoyt, who never forgot the incident, was able to cap the tale by ordering the schooner *Stella* designed by Alden, recalling the 1901 incident in the letter placing the order.

The little sloop finally made Sakonnet after a twenty-one-day odyssey, and the young sailor had picked up much of the practical knowledge he was later to put to such good use.

It is an interesting coincidence that Alden had the same brush with formal education as Olin Stephens would some years later, at the beginning of his career. The Alden family wanted John to study naval architecture at M.I.T., but he was so

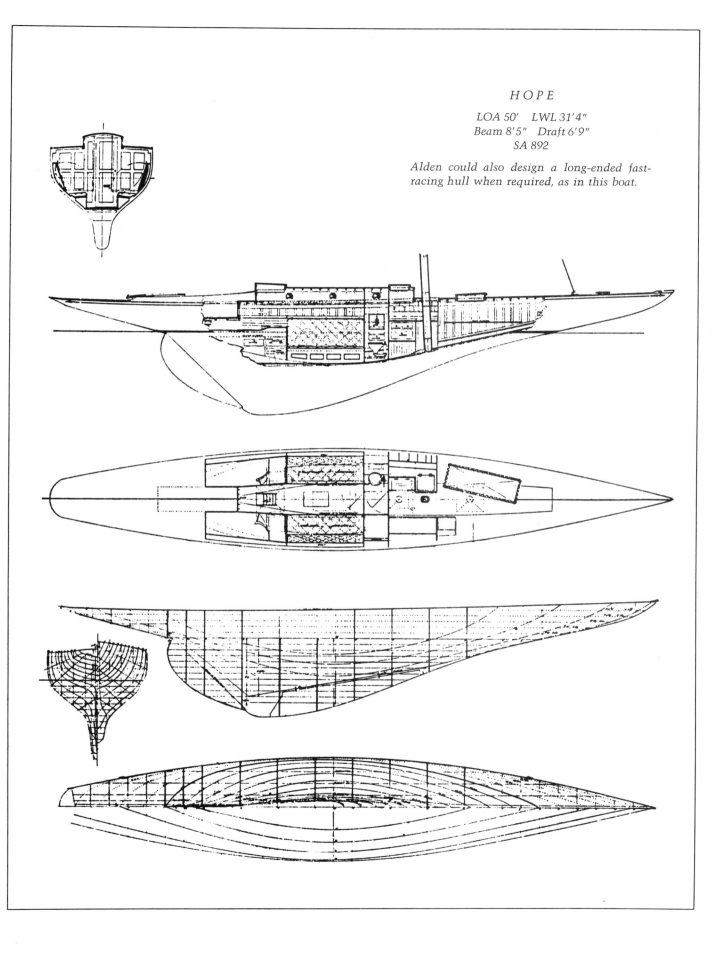

HOPE

LOA 50'   LWL 31'4"
Beam 8'5"   Draft 6'9"
SA 892

Alden could also design a long-ended fast-racing hull when required, as in this boat.

eager to get to work that, instead of entering college, he started in the Boston office of B. B. Crowninshield. John later took courses at M.I.T. to fill himself in on some technical areas, but his basic "education" was simply his own feel for a boat and how she should accommodate to the sea.

Crowninshield was turning out the long-ended, low freeboard racing yachts typical of the day, fine for an afternoon around the buoys but not intended for deep water. However, the yacht designer also had shares in a fishing schooner named *Fame*. In December 1908, she had to be ferried from Halifax, where she was stranded by legal difficulties, to Boston, and John volunteered to join a small crew sent there for the task. To get her away they had to slip out of the harbor at night, with only four able-bodied hands aboard a vessel that usually required over twenty in crew, straight into a winter blizzard. It blew them out into the Gulf Stream and, eventually, all the way down to the Jersey coast. This rugged experience might have sent some people back to Troy for good, or even further west into farm country, but for Alden it was a significant milestone in his life. Through it he gained great respect for the sea-keeping qualities and capabilities of the fisherman type of hull. This voyage was more of an education than most designers could get in years of taking courses.

The fisherman type, in contrast to the shallow, long-ended, relatively flat-bottomed hulls that were then popular for yacht racing, was deep and full, with short but graceful ends and a long keel. It developed through years of practical experience on the offshore fishing banks, where a boat was required to stay out for weeks, supporting a large crew in all kinds of weather. Then, with a full load of fish aboard, she had to have the sailing ability to reach the market fast in order to obtain the best possible price for the catch.

When Alden saw how *Fame* survived the beating she took on that winter voyage, and began to appreciate the ease with which her husky, able hull adapted to the waves instead of "fighting" them, he started to develop theories and ideas on using the type for yachts. He enjoyed offshore sailing himself, and he reasoned that other ardent yachtsmen would like the experience too if they only had a suitable boat. Even for coastal cruising in the rough chop of Buzzards Bay and Nantucket Sound, or in the exposed waters of the Gulf of Maine, the type would do very well for yacht use, as Alden saw it. When he opened his own office in 1909, design No. 1 was a clipper-bowed sloop that did not embody these characteristics and was, reportedly, an indifferent sailer. However, the fisherman schooner soon began to appear as a yacht in a style so distinctive that any knowledgeable sailor of the era could look at one and instantly say "Alden." Its essential characteristics included the deep, full-bodied hull and short overhangs, with graceful counter and spoon

Sea Gypsy, *at 78 feet, was one of Alden's larger schooners.*

Above, Fayaway, *a typical small Alden cruising boat of the 1930s*

Left, Traveler II *(ex* Quail*) was a familiar charter yacht in the Bahamas for many years.*

QUAIL

LOA 68'2" LWL 52'8"
Beam 18' Draft 5'9"
SA 1666

A beamy centerboarder with great sail-carry-ing ability and a great amount of room, she became the popular charter yacht Traveler II.

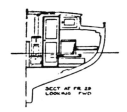

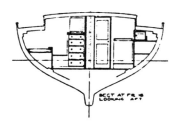

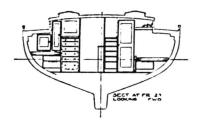

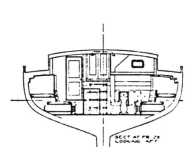

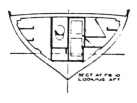

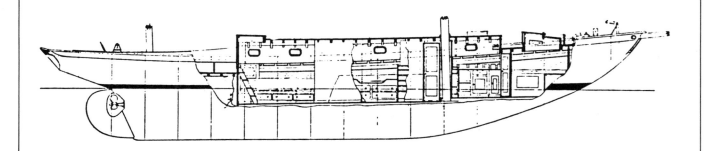

bow, and a long keel and good-sized rudder under the after end of the waterline. There was wetted surface in abundance, cutting down on light-weather performance, but the ability to adapt to sea conditions offshore was the key. Most of them were rigged with gaff foresail and main and topsails, though he occasionally went to a Marconi main in later years. The keel configuration could also be changed to a centerboard model for those requiring it.

In the years before World War I, Alden schooners began to appear in all yachting areas, but it wasn't until after the wartime break, when Alden did some designing for the government, that they really came to dominate the yachting scene. John was his own best salesman, and the success of his firm owed almost as much to his business acumen as it did to his abilities as designer and sailor. He established relationships with many small yards in Maine that had made their living for years building commercial sailing vessels and were in need of other work now that commercial sail was going into a decline. Alden managed to achieve quality and economy as an attractive package in his dealings with these yards, and he also established a stock name for his personal boats that was to become as famous and familiar as his own name and almost synonymous with it.

This stock name was Malabar. John had thirteen yachts by that name before he retired from designing in 1955 and sold his business, and the way he sailed them and campaigned them was vital to the reputation they built up. For a 41-foot, 3-inch schooner he had built in 1921 he picked the name as an appropriately salty one from the old explorers' charts of Cape Cod. What is now known as Monomoy Point at the bottom tip of the Cape's "elbow" was once listed as Malabar. The first *Malabar* was a very plain, simple boat with bald-headed gaff rig and club-footed working jib, designed to be a singlehander. He wanted to dramatize their simplicity for cruising and passaging, and the first three *Malabar*s were built with this wish in mind. Each was used by Alden for a season and then sold, and, as the years went on and their reputations became better known, prospective buyers were literally waiting at the dock when John completed his spring delivery voyage back from Maine. The early ones were all schooners, but there was one yawl and the last two were ketches.

An outgrowth of the interest in these schooners was a move to revive ocean racing to show what they were capable of. Offshore racing had been done on a luxury basis with paid crews, for the most part, but it had never become firmly established and was completely halted by World War I. To foster interest in offshore work, the Bermuda Race was revived in 1923, and *Malabar IV*, a more sophisticated 46-footer than the first three, gave Alden and the type of boat a giant push into the limelight by winning. His designs took three of the first five places, the race caught on with yachtsmen, and Alden fisherman schooners became the dominant type in the next nine years of the race's history as well as in many other areas. John won it again in 1926 with *Malabar VII* and set a record that has been matched, but not beaten, by winning a third time in 1932 with *Malabar X*. The 1932 winner was the supreme development of the fisherman type as an offshore racer, a 58-footer with 1635 feet of sail in a lofty rig with main, topsail, and fisherman, as well as a full complement of headsails. It was a fast-reaching race, real schooner weather, and the *"Ten"* really flew down the course, along with three of her sisters. Alden schooners took the top four corrected places.

Alden boats won the Transpac three times, including actor Frank Morgan's victory in the schooner *Dolphin II* in 1947, and Alden had won prizes in other *Malabar*s in intervening Bermuda years, but his supreme achievement was the sweep of the '32 race. Alden boats still figured prominently in later years, and he designed new yawls and sloops that remained with the modern trend. *Mandoo II*, now *Royono*, a 71-foot yawl, was one of the best, and she and *Malabar X*, incidentally, were familiar for years to southern charter yacht customers.

Under the press of competition, and in an attempt to catch up with the fame Alden had gained by his dominance of offshore racing for ten years, boats were designed that would rate well under the handicapping formula then in use and be fast and able offshore—without possessing the rugged characteristics Alden boats inherited from their fisherman forebears. Alden, too, went along with these ideas, as he was far from set in his ways in an addiction to one type of boat. The popular demand for a boat to outperform his able schooners resulted in the victory of the Olin Stephens-designed *Edlu* in 1934 and Philip Rhodes's *Kirawan* in 1936. The Stephens-designed *Baruna*'s 1938 win marked the end of an era and established the trend away from the husky schooner type to narrower, long-ended yawls and sloops. Moreover, they were designed especially to the measurement rule, and the schooners had not been.

When there was work hard on the wind, these boats were closer-winded and faster than the schooners, but old-timers will tell you that there wasn't anything quite like the thrill of one of John o' Boston's big schooners surging toward Bermuda with everything set in a fresh southwester and John himself tweaking a guy here, freeing a sheet there, and calling for an occasional headsail change to keep her charging along at her best.

This influence on ocean racing was only one of the facets of John Alden's domination of yachting in the twenties and thirties. The schooner design had been crystallized into a near-stock 43-footer, either keel or centerboard, that was turned

Malabar X, *winner of the 1932 Bermuda Race, marked the peak of success of the fisherman-type schooner in offshore racing.*

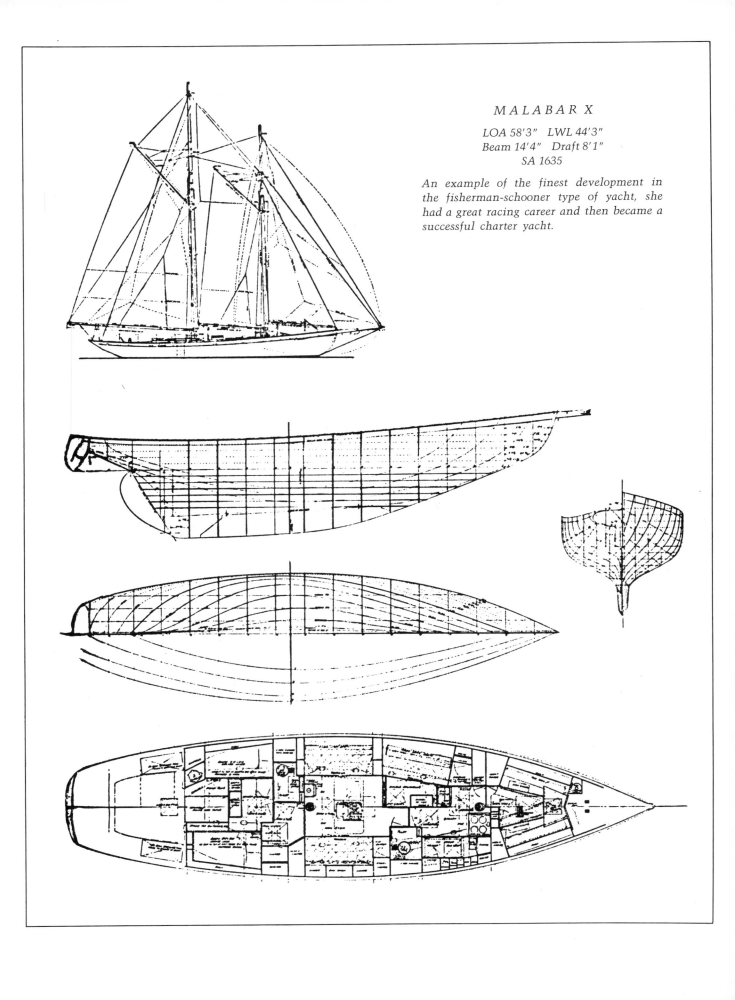

MALABAR X

LOA 58'3"   LWL 44'3"
Beam 14'4"   Draft 8'1"
SA 1635

An example of the finest development in the fisherman-schooner type of yacht, she had a great racing career and then became a successful charter yacht.

out by the dozens in Maine shipyards. Often they were built on speculation ahead of owners' orders by the Alden office, but they seldom went begging, even when the Depression of the early thirties caught John with several unsold boats under construction in his favorite Maine yards. The 43-footers can still be seen in many cruising harbors today, many tended with loving care by owners who are proud of their traditional look and feel. Alden also capitalized on the Malabar name with a small cruising cutter known as the Malabar Jr. Class. It started as a gaff-rigged 30-footer in 1925 and went through many updatings into the 1950s, with close to 100 turned out altogether.

Two other Alden designs were extremely influential in popularizing cruising in medium-sized auxiliaries, and they also did well in coastal racing and some off-shore work. These were the 36-foot Coastwise Cruiser, which seemed to fill a very strong need of the late thirties for a moderate-cost boat that could cruise a family comfortably and still race, and the 42-foot Off Soundings yawl. Alden was a charter member of the Cruising Club of America and believed as much in its fostering of healthy cruising boats as he did in its sponsorship of the Bermuda Race. Both of these types are still very much in evidence in major areas. About 20 per cent of his firm's business was in powerboats, but he turned most of that work over to assistants.

Small-boat sailing in the fresh southwesters of Buzzards Bay out of Sakonnet had always been one of Alden's favorite pastimes, and this was reflected in his many day-sailing one-design classes. Most were designed and manufactured before the days of mass production of nationally distributed classes with officers, governing bodies, constitutions, class championships, and all the paraphernalia of present-day competition in this field. They were often designed for one club and its special local conditions, and a class in one area could have a slightly different version in other locales. The O boat, originally designed in 1921, was typical of this. Massachusetts Bay Indians, Triangles, U.S. One-Designs, X Class frostbite dinghies, and many more came from the Alden board. His own last boat was the Sakonnet Class 18½-footer, turned out especially for his home club, in which he spent his later years on the same waters where he had learned to sail. Occasionally he turned out a bigger "racing machine" but his heart wasn't really in this type. Some of his Q and R boats did well, and the 66-foot *Sachem,* first a schooner built to the Universal Rule, later a sloop, was known as his "racingest" boat and won many cups in afternoon events around the buoys and on squadron and club runs.

When Alden retired in 1955, selling the business to an Alden owner, Donald Parrot, he had turned out close to 1000 designs (the record is not exactly clear), and

Above, Malabar XIII *was the last of Alden's famous* Malabars.

Right, Minot's Light, *a good example*
of Alden's postwar work

four or five times that number of boats, many built from one set of plans, were representing John Alden afloat.

Although the big schooners—built of wood, with cotton sails and the deep sea-kindly underbodies of a boat meant to go to sea and stay there for months as a home and working platform for a big crew—are no longer a major part of the yachting scene, everybody who goes to sea in an offshore racer or a comfortable coastal cruising boat owes at least a partial debt to salty John o' Boston and all he did, through the basic soundness of the boats he designed, to make possible today's great popularity of both these facets of the sport.

Left, stately 83-foot Serena *was a top competitor on the Pacific coast into the 1970s.*

Philip L. Rhodes

Five

Philip L. Rhodes

Some yacht designers only do one thing well, others are a bit more versatile, but noted for a specialty, and a few can lend their touch to almost anything that floats. Perhaps the best-known example of the versatile approach is Philip L. Rhodes. This stocky, curly-haired Ohioan began designing yachts in the 1920s, and the roster of Rhodes designs ranges over an enormous gamut of success stories unmatched in the field for variety and contrast in one body of work.

From the 11-foot Penguin racing dinghy, over 9000 strong throughout the world with about 7500 in the U.S., to the Cup defender *Weatherly,* from the Dyer D dinghy to Bermuda Race winners like *Kirawan* and *Carina,* from small launches to 140-foot luxury yachts, plus cargo ships, naval vessels, hydrofoils, and racing powerboats—Rhodes has turned out an incredible inventory of designs. Anybody with a modicum of interest in any form of yachting is familiar with at least several Rhodes designs, has certainly been aboard some, and will perhaps be surprised to learn about some others. Even when he was well into his seventies, Rhodes continued to turn them out prolifically.

All this stems from an unlikely background for someone whose production of designs has made his name a byword wherever yachtsmen meet. This distinguished nautically oriented career had its beginnings in the Ohio River Valley.

Born in Thurman, Ohio, in 1895, the son of a carriage maker, Rhodes grew up in the river town of Gallipolis. As a boy, he acquired an early fascination with the steamboat traffic on the river, the thumping paddles, the bright lights, the hoot of whistles, and the magic blare of distant calliopes. Before high school, the family moved to Newark, Ohio, near Buckeye Lake. Young Phil had already started drawing and sketching boats, and the small boats on the lake caught his eye. He seldom did much boating himself, however, though he once had a summer job at an amusement park tending small U-drive power launches—nautical versions of "Dodgems"—and spent most of the time fending off the crash landings of the customers.

Basketball was actually his favorite sport in high school and at Denison University. The preoccupation with drawing boats remained, however, and after two years he transferred to M.I.T. in Cambridge, Massachusetts, with a friend who wanted to study engineering. As an undergraduate, Rhodes became a paid assistant to Professor George Owen, whose courses in naval architecture and yacht design were the most influential in the field at the time. One of Rhodes's early assignments was a study of the lines of an Owen catboat.

The Rhodes academic career ended in September 1918, as World War I neared its close. He had already enlisted in the Army Engineers and went into training at Boston Navy Yard preparatory to being sent to France as a naval constructor. The Armistice changed this prospect, and he returned to Ohio, perhaps because his future wife was a supervisor of kindergartens in Cleveland. He went to work as a shipfitter in a Lorain boatyard and is proud of the fact that he is the only yacht designer he knows who holds a shipwright's card.

The next step was to train as an apprentice with Union Shipbuilding Company in Baltimore, from which post he went on to New York as a married man and as the company's representative there. When the postwar cutbacks caught up with the shipbuilding business, Rhodes went into mechanical engineering for a while. However, he had never stopped drawing yacht designs, and he decided to try to find some customers for what had been his own daydreams up to that point. In 1924 he rented a hole-in-the-wall office in New York for $60 a month, inserted the smallest ads that *Yachting* magazine would take, and began to pick up a few contracts.

His first boat to make *Yachting*'s Design Section was a 30-foot auxiliary offered with three alternate rigs—gaff yawl, gaff sloop, and Marconi cutter. The plans appeared in June 1925, and the commentary stated that she was a sound boat "not extreme in any direction...able yet yachty." An in-depth article in July 1927 discussed his design of *Tidal Wave*, an adaptation for Sam Wetherill, then the magazine's Associate Editor. She was developed from a well-known double-

Tidal Wave *stirred great interest in 1930
and was highly successful in races.*

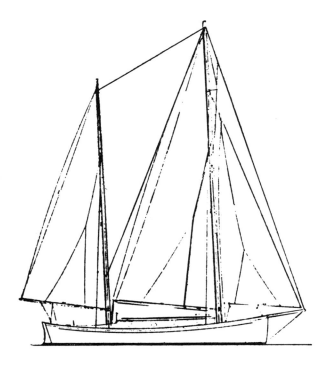

TIDAL WAVE

LOA 32'4"   LWL 31'
Beam 11'   Draft 5'
SA 650

*A development of the Block Island cat-rigged
schooners, she was a new idea in 1930 for
a small racing-cruising yacht and won more
than her share of races.*

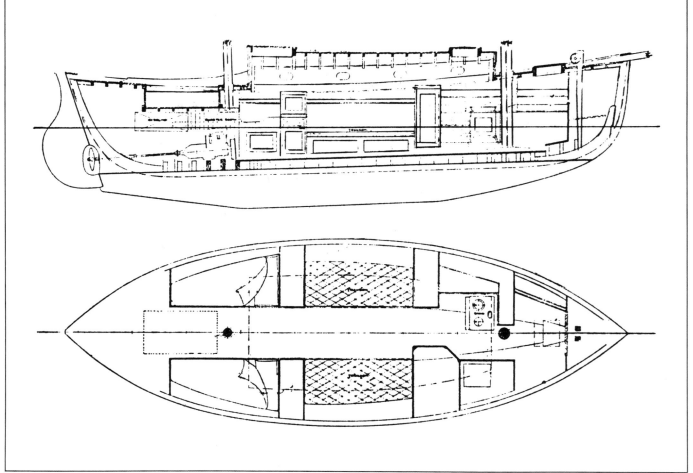

ended centerboarder, *West Island,* which Wetherill had owned for a while. *West Island* was a descendant of the Block Island schooner type, a cat-schooner with gaff rig, and Wetherill wanted some of her good qualities combined with additional ideas. Rhodes made *Tidal Wave* a keelboat and gave her a Marconi ketch rig, and she proved a fine combination of comfort and sailing ability, winning her share of races. Wetherill wrote several articles about her, and she became one of the best-known boats in the area. (She is still in good condition at Three-Mile Harbor, Long Island, and acquired a new owner in the early seventies.)

The Rhodes versatility was demonstrated at this early stage by a stock 45-foot cabin cruiser for the M. M. Davis Company of Maryland and a fast, twin-screw commuter, and the commissions began to come in more frequently. In fact, Rhodes was able to take on assistants from time to time, and some of them became well-known names in the field, such as Winthrop Warner and Henry Devereux. Perhaps most interestingly, for one short period of a week or two a young teen-age hopeful named Olin Stephens, soon to settle permanently into a partnership with Drake Sparkman, worked in the Rhodes office.

The first Rhodes ocean racer to gain some attention was *Ayesha,* a 46-foot yawl, that fresh from the builder's yard, debuted in the 1932 Bermuda Race. With the Alden influence very strong in that era, it was thought that centerboarders were not suitable for offshore work. They were all right for gunkhole cruising in shallow coastal areas, but offshore work required a deep hull. Rhodes went against this thinking because the boat was to be used in shallow water areas as well as deep water ones, and he also felt that a shallow, beamy hull could have excellent sail-carrying abilities. That it could also go to windward when designed properly was proved by *Ayesha.* The 1932 race was a hard thrash, close-hauled on starboard tack, in which *Highland Light* set a course record that lasted twenty-four years; but *Ayesha* surprised traditionalists by taking third in Class B. When her plans appeared in the August *Yachting,* the introductory comment was that "it is rare for a moderate draft centerboarder to make a good showing, and even rarer for one to earn raves from her crew."

Further comment from this analysis of her could almost be used as a standard text for describing a "typical" Rhodes boat over all the years of his productivity. "Her lines and sections show clearly what a sweet craft she is, with firm yet easy sections, moderate deadrise, sweeping sheer, nicely proportioned ends and good freeboard. The buttocks and diagonals are unusually easy for a shoal, rather wide hull."

Although well ahead of his day in promoting centerboarders for ocean racing, Rhodes wasn't restricted to the type. *Narada,* designed in 1936 for Corrin Strong,

Escapade *proved a big centerboarder could be fast.*
She swept the Great Lakes on several occasions
and broke the Miami-Nassau record in 1966,
late in her career.

was a keel 46-footer and a pre-sister of *Carina*, which was built in 1946 and in which Dick Nye won the 1952 Bermuda Race. Strong later became U.S. Ambassador to Norway and sailed *Narada* across for use there.

In 1936 Rhodes also had his first Bermuda winner, Robert Baruch's *Kirawan*, a 53-foot keel cutter that was third to finish in a record fleet of forty-three in very rough going. Rhodes was in the crew, sunburned and smiling when he stepped ashore in Bermuda and found only two bigger boats in the harbor—and the bigger *Stormy Weather*, hot boat of the era after her Transatlantic win, a few miles astern.

Although he sailed as often as possible and was always a key member of any crew he was in, Rhodes's passion for detail, and for working on even the most minor items himself, kept him at his board for long hours. He did find time to cruise with his family on occasion and in later years was able to relax aboard the fast aluminum cruiser *Touche* he had designed.

By 1934 he had moved into the celebrated firm of Cox and Stevens, in charge of yacht design, and was head of a staff that had grown to about fifteen by the end of the decade. Even with a big staff, Rhodes did much of the work that some designers delegate to junior assistants.

Ocean racing was really beginning to build up as the country emerged from the depths of the Depression, and the big names of the era were John Alden, Rhodes, and Stephens. Each year new designs from their boards were awaited with great interest, and the competition afloat gained a new pace and intensity.

Among the many boats that Rhodes turned out in this era, *Alondra* (1937), *Escapade* (1938), and *Kirawan II* (1938) were some of the best known. *Alondra*, built for a man who had been *Ayesha*'s owner previously, gained her greatest fame as *Caribbee* under Carleton Mitchell and Seabury Stanton. Mitchell, who cruised her extensively in North America and Scandinavia and raced her with great success, developed a fondness for centerboarders from the experience.

Escapade, built for Henry Fownes and later campaigned extensively by Wendell Anderson of Detroit, carried "centerboard thinking" up to the 72-foot top limit of ocean racers. Over the years she built up one of the notable records in the sport, sweeping Great Lakes events several times; as late as 1966 she managed to break *Ticonderoga*'s twenty-six-year-old record in the Miami-Nassau Race, shaving off three minutes for a 19:33:37 clocking for the 176 nautical miles, while under charter to Robert Way of Erie, Pennsylvania.

Kirawan II was built for Baruch in an attempt to repeat his Bermuda success. She never did this, but as Paul Hoffman's *Hother* she had many years of racing success. Rhodes originally designed her with a short bowsprit to get the optimum fore-triangle, but then he decided that the sprit didn't look right and added a

Left, widely traveled Caribbee *was a successful racer
and a fine cruising boat.*

Maruffa *achieved her greatest fame
in the Pacific Northwest.*

One of the later Rhodes ocean racers was the distinctive
Thunderhead, *shown here nearing Bermuda in 1964.*

clipper bow instead. This distinctive touch made her an easy boat to identify, and Hoffman had it repeated when Rhodes designed *Thunderhead* for him in 1962. Under Hoffman, *Hother* took twenty-nine prizes in thirty-three races.

Switching from ocean racers, Rhodes turned out the 11-foot Penguin design in 1939, and the first fleet was built by a Washington, D.C., group. She was intended to provide an able dinghy for club and college sailing that could be constructed inexpensively by home builders or in cooperative programs, and she filled the bill so well that the class is still one of the strongest one-design groups in organized competition. Following the ordinary practice of that era, when a few dozen boats seemed like a big class, Rhodes sold the plans outright to the young and struggling class association, ironically thus losing royalties on 9000 boats. The next popular one-design from his board was the 13½-foot Wood Pussy catboat in 1944, a class that is still organized, and these early successes were followed by such popular types as the Bantam, Rhodes 18, and Rhodes 19 in keel and centerboard versions. The Rhodes 19 is one of the most widespread and well-organized classes today, with close to 2000 boats and especially popular with those who like to combine good racing with comfortable day sailing.

The gathering tensions of the late thirties and early forties brought Rhodes and his office more and more into government work. With the advent of World War II all efforts went into military contracts, and the staff increased until Rhodes headed an office with more than 500 employees. The work here ranged from small military launches to conversion of such liners as *America, Manhattan,* and *Normandie.* Transports, patrol craft, sub chasers, minelayers, and many other specialized types were all in the picture. Over a hundred 185-foot minesweepers were built.

The end of the war saw the dissolution of Cox and Stevens. Rhodes was back on his own with a greatly increased staff over the prewar years, and there was an immediate return to yacht work. The pressures of long-deferred dreams that had been held up during the war years brought a tremendous amount of new work to yacht designers. In addition to developing new ocean racers, Rhodes began to turn out a distinctive type of motorsailer (or full-powered auxiliary, depending upon anyone's choice of words). *Windjammer II* for Garner Tullis of New Orleans, a 77-foot shoal draft ketch with center cockpit, was the forerunner of a design that included such well-known boats as *Dragon Lady* and *Velila. Curlew III* (98 feet) and *Sea Prince* (82 feet) were larger versions of this type, and the use of some of the features went into the powerful ocean-racing, cruising ketch *Barlovento II,* Pierre S. duPont III's 72-footer. Not at her best in light going, *Barlovento* could really get moving in a breeze, and she ran away with such events as the snow-blown Storm

Right, Weatherly *was the successful America's Cup defender in 1962. She is the only Rhodes 12-Meter.*

Thousands of Penguin dinghies have provided exciting one-design action in many waters.

Caper on her way to a Bermuda Race Class prize in 1964

Trysail Race in 1961 and the several heavy-weather Skipper Races in the Chesapeake. In the storm-tossed 1960 Bermuda Race, she charged up from far back in the fleet after a period of light calms as the only boat to carry a full main through the 60-knot blow, finishing seventh overall and fourth in Class A in an awesome display of power and stability.

La Belle Sole, Bar-L-Rick, Fei-Seen, and *Virginia Reel* were other motorsailers that had a strong influence on later boats of the same general type, and an unusual assignment was the adaptation of the Thames River Barge type to a 100-foot yacht, *Rara Avis,* for Paul Hammond. *Rara Avis* was indeed a rare bird, but in all the cruising boats whose lines really came from his board, and were not adaptations, there was a distinctive combination of good looks and a great amount of comfort with real sailing ability. Rhodes hulls always seemed to accommodate well to the sea and had the feeling of a real ship about them even when they were relatively small.

Irving Pratt's graceful blue 56-foot sloop *Caper* (1958) was one of Rhodes's more successful ocean-racing designs of the forties and fifties, but it was Dick Nye in the two *Carina*s who brought Rhodes designs their greatest ocean-racing glory. In 1952, the first *Carina* won the Bermuda Race, the first Class C boat ever to do so, and the next year, campaigning in England, she won the Cowes-Dinard, Cross Channel, and Britannia Cup, plus a class second in the Fastnet. She also won such U.S. events as the Halifax, Vineyard, Block Island, and Bayview-Mackinac races. As *Chee Chee V,* and at age twenty-four, this veteran campaigner took Class B honors and fourth in fleet in the 1970 St. Pete–Fort Lauderdale Race.

Nye, who came to ocean racing with a late start as a rank novice at the age of forty-two in 1945, really had the bug after *Carina*'s successes and turned to Rhodes for his next boat in 1955. In thinking back over all of his designs, Rhodes admits that perhaps his greatest affection is for this second *Carina,* and her record would certainly make anyone proud. She had two Transatlantic Race victories (Sweden in '55 and Spain in '57, a first in the sport), two Fastnet wins in contrasting conditions of light airs the first time and a rugged gale the second, and a whole host of wins in lesser races, plus Bermuda Race class prizes.

She was a combination keel-centerboarder with a good beam of 13 feet, a lead-ballasted keel giving her good displacement, and a bronze board. A yawl with seven-eighths fore-triangle, she was 53½ by 36¼ feet with 1164 feet of sail.

At the height of Rhodes's success as an ocean-racing designer, the America's Cup revival in 1958 gave him his first chance at a Cup defender design, and his first 12-Meter. The syndicate headed by Henry Mercer ordered *Weatherly* from Rhodes, and as a late starter in 1958 she never became fully shaken down before

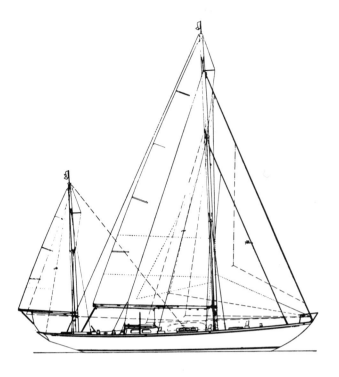

CARINA

LOA 53'6"   LWL 36'3"
Beam 13'   Draft 6'
SA 1194

This powerful centerboarder, with great sail-carrying ability, was Rhodes's choice as his favorite of all his designs.

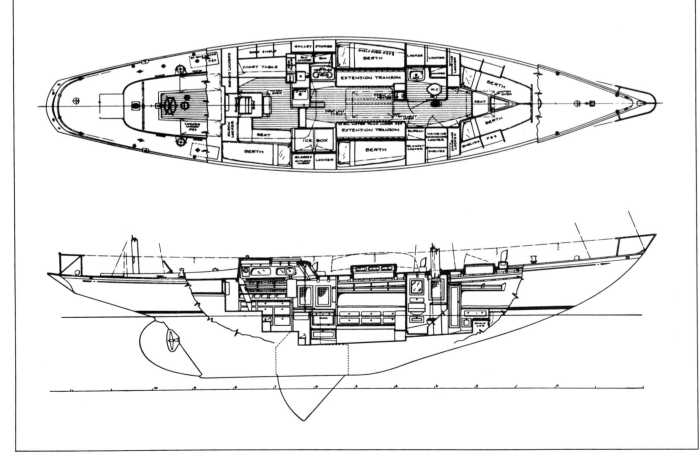

Carina, *twice a Transatlantic winner*

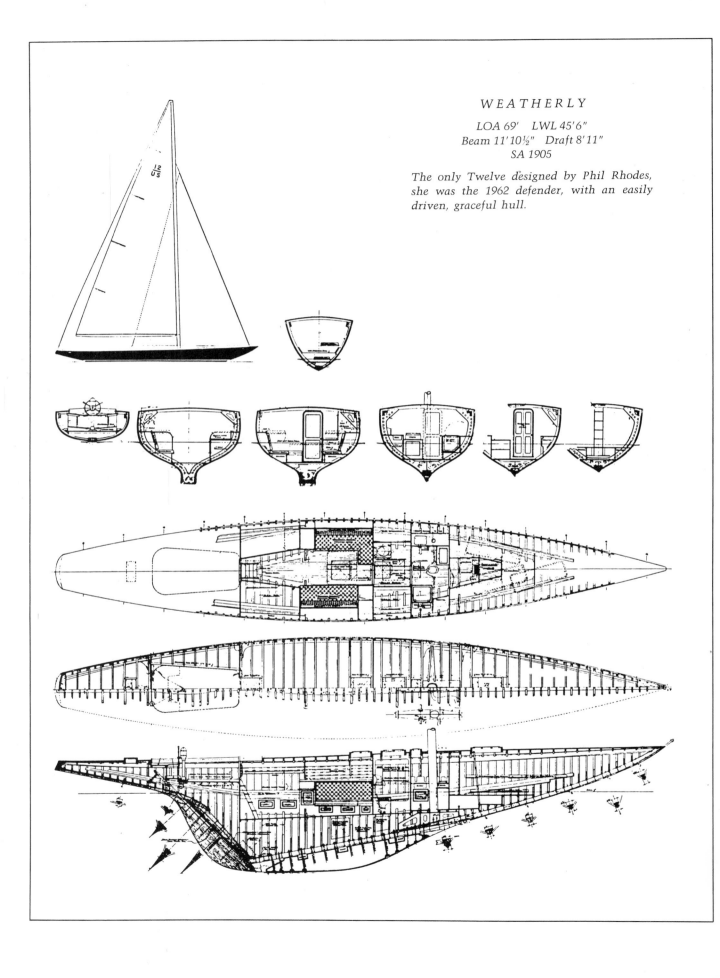

WEATHERLY

LOA 69' LWL 45'6"
Beam 11'10½" Draft 8'11"
SA 1905

The only Twelve designed by Phil Rhodes,
she was the 1962 defender, with an easily
driven, graceful hull.

she was eliminated by *Columbia.* Few Cup boats are ever given a second chance, but *Weatherly* was in the 1962 campaign. Consultations with Bill Luders, at whose yard she had been built, brought about some changes aimed at weight reduction above the water and consequent increase in ballast, plus other refinements. With Bus Mosbacher and a well-drilled crew giving her a good ride, the results became history: selection over the new *Nefertiti* and *Columbia,* which had beaten her in 1958, and an exciting 4–1 win over the Australian *Gretel.*

Rhodes had an important influence in another quite different phase of the sport, the swing to fiberglass construction for stock cruising auxiliaries. Back in 1939 he had produced the Bounty design for a low-cost family cruising boat with good performance characteristics. This 38-foot sloop with accommodations for four was an entry into a category that had recently become popular—the easily handled cruising boat for a small family. The Alden Coastwise Cruiser and the Sparkman and Stephens Week-Ender were similar in concept; Bounty offered just a bit more room and, being a bit bigger, an improvement in sailing characteristics. It seems incredible that this boat, with a 25-horsepower inboard engine, was listed at a base price of $3875 at the 1940 Motor Boat Show. The low price was made possible by mass production techniques, and she was a sensation. Unfortunately, however, the sensation was short-lived, as World War II ended all pleasure-boat building just when the Bounty was beginning to gain a reputation.

After the war, and the emergence of fiberglass as a boatbuilding material, the same people who had promoted the wooden Rhodes Bounty before the war, Coleman Boat Company, decided to go into stock production of a fiberglass auxiliary; again they came to Rhodes. The old Bounty design was lengthened to 40 feet and changed a bit for fiberglass construction, and the rig was modernized. It proved well suited to the new material, and the new Bounty was the most-talked-about boat at the 1957 Boat Show in New York. The class had a good racing record, and this concept led the way toward the complete "fiberglass revolution" that soon followed.

Rhodes had other designs that were important in establishing the trend to fiberglass, such as the Ranger 28, Swiftsure, Vanguard, and Reliant—all popular auxiliaries. In addition, the Penguin, Rhodes 19, Wood Pussy, and Bantam were among the one-designs from Rhodes's board that were adapted to fiberglass.

And then, by way of contrast from this man of many contrasts, one of Rhodes's later designs was the unusual and stately 122-foot steel three-masted ketch *Sea Star,* built by Goudy and Stevens of East Boothbay, Maine, for Laurance Rockefeller. Manned by a crew of nine, she has deluxe accommodations for a party of ten and was especially designed for Caribbean charter operations when not being

The 122-foot, three-masted ketch Sea Star built for the Rockefeller family is a distinctive, unusual yacht from Rhodes's board.

One of the largest motor yachts built in the 1960s
was the 164-foot Pilgrim.

*Phil Rhodes found relaxation when possible
on* Touche, *from his own designs.*

used by her owner. Once again, an outstanding and unusual boat exhibited the Rhodes flair for combining comfort and ability. Following her off the design board was the aluminum twin-screw motor yacht *Manu Kai,* at 130 feet one of the largest yachts built in recent years.

And so the Rhodes designs poured out prolifically. Such has been the range of his accomplishments that it isn't hard to imagine a harbor completely populated by boats from Rhodes's board—from dinghy to 140-foot motor yacht, with no type of pleasure boat missing from the scene.

Editor's Note: Philip Rhodes died at the age of seventy-nine on August 29, 1974.

William H. Tripp

Six

Bill Tripp

Many people flounder around for years in search of their true métier, while others, a rarer breed, know from a very early age exactly what they want to do when they grow up. A classic example of the latter group was William H. Tripp, a native Long Islander from the suburbs of New York, who started sketching boat designs in his preteen years and kept at it with complete dedication from then on. When he died in an automobile accident at the age of fifty-one in 1971, twenty years after he put out his own shingle, Tripp was one of the best-known and most influential of modern yacht designers.

As a youngster in Bayside, Long Island, on the shores of Little Neck Bay, Bill spent hours looking at the boats in the bay, always "thought boats," and went out on the water as much as possible. When a siege of strep throat confined him to bed for a long time, he kept himself busy by drawing boat designs, and he never really stopped. While the early ones drawn in bed might perhaps have been of interest only to fond parents and a few friends, a new Tripp design at the height of his career had an immediate impact on hundreds of potential owners of stock auxiliaries and on the ocean-racing fleets of the world.

It was not long before Bill progressed from the idle sketching and dreaming stage to some practical applications. As a teen-ager he was racing in the Star Class and designing several rig alterations; he also found time to do some conversion plans for cruising boats.

Eager to get into designing, like several others of the more successful designers today, he took a job as an apprentice rather than wait out the slower process of a formal education. For two years he worked in the office of Philip L. Rhodes. Two boats he remembered working on were *Cherry Blossom* and *Narada*. The latter, a 46-foot sloop, was a pre-sister of the *Carina* in which Dick Nye won the 1952 Bermuda Race.

Tripp, tall and gangling, with a shock of blond hair, a ready grin on a round face, and brown eyes surrounded by smile crinkles, continued to sail as much as possible, gaining experience afloat, and it wasn't long before he had the chance for some really intensive experience. With World War II fast approaching, he joined the Coast Guard and was assigned to the Offshore Patrol out of Greenport, Long Island. This very special branch of the service created some enduring legends —as well as some of today's best-known sailors—with its all-weather, all-seasons operations on the lookout for subs approaching our shores in the early days of the war. With conventional antisubmarine vessels in short supply, sailing yachts were used as lookout posts, their only defense a machine gun or two and the difficulty of detecting them due to the silence of operating under sail. There was no better school for finding out how the hull of a sailing vessel acts in a sea, and Bill found the firsthand encounter a valuable experience. He was also proud of the fact that he did some duty on the square-rigged ship *Danmark* when the Coast Guard took her over from the Danes, and he smilingly claimed to be the only modern yacht designer with a square-rigger background. Before the war ended, he had gone on to the Pacific, where he was a navigator of an LST.

Back to civilian life, and more determined than ever to become a yacht designer, he joined Sparkman and Stephens for a while, doing some work on PT-boat designs; in 1952, he finally took the big jump into solo practice. In 1950, he had had his first design printed in the Design Section of *Yachting*, a 39-foot keel-centerboard sloop that he designed for a contest run by the British magazine *Yachting World*. The design took second prize out of more than forty entries, and *Yachting*'s commentary in presenting it to U.S. readers was that it was encouraging to see the design do so well in England, where there had been great emphasis on light displacement developments at the time, when Tripp's was for a moderately conventional boat.

Before 1950 was over, Tripp designs for a 25-foot semistock fast cruiser built at the Knutson yard on Long Island, and a 47-foot moderate-displacement ocean-racing yawl had been published, and the following year saw two stock cruisers

*The Medalist Class, displaying such Tripp trademarks as a wide transom,
high freeboard, and strong sheer, was one of the early stock designs
in her size range, just over 30 feet, to do well in competition.*

and the design for the Resolute Class one-design sloop appear. A significant step forward in the Tripp career was *Katingo,* designed for Captain John Vatis as an entry in the 1956 Bermuda Race, with Tripp in the afterguard. She had been extensively tank-tested and was in the current trend of beamy centerboarders. She also had a secret weapon, a quadrilateral mizzen staysail. *Katingo* didn't burn up the course, and she was not extensively campaigned, but she had attracted a lot of attention, and some of the ideas were adapted into subsequently developed designs that made their mark competitively as well.

In 1957, the 48-foot flush-deck sloop *Touche,* built for John Potter of Seawanhaka Corinthian Yacht Club, made her appearance, and she became one of those "landmark" boats that set a trend in general while generating a durable and distinguished racing career of their own. She was built of double-planked mahogany over oak frames at Abeking and Rasmussen in Germany and arrived just in time for the New York Yacht Club cruise, where she turned in a 11–1–2–3 record. She represented a lot of original thinking in a designer-owner collaboration, with midship cockpits to port and starboard, pivoting steering pedestal that could be adjusted athwartships so the helmsman could keep his eye on the genoa luff, sliding chart table, an off-center Mercedes diesel, a centerboard trunk below the cabin sole, and many other unusual features. In a long and successful career, during which she was taken over by Dr. Herbert Virgin of Florida, she won one race and was fourth in the series standings as late as the 1969 SORC. She remained a threat in all events until the change to the IOR hurt her.

In *Touche,* Bill concentrated on keeping weight amidships and on low wetted surface, items that weren't as frequently considered in those days as they are now. Her bulbous underwater lines, suggested to him somewhat by the atomic submarines, as well as the heavy, foil-type centerboard blade, were considered to be startling innovations in many quarters.

While developing these ideas, Bill had also been keeping track of the inroads of fiberglass in the pleasure boat field, and he began to think seriously about using the material for ocean racers. It was difficult to get test data on it as supplied to this special field, so he set about doing his own testing. Some of his methods, in the absence of fancy facilities, were crude but effective. To test the resiliency and strength of fiberglass panels, for example, he placed them in his driveway and drove the car over them; gradually he gained enough confidence to go ahead with plans for a 40-foot yawl. Originally known as the Vitesse Class, it went through some switches of sponsorship and eventually emerged as the Block Island 40, another design whose success had a tremendous influence, and which also

Touche, which had a long winning career far beyond the expectancy of most ocean racers, embodied many radical ideas when she first appeared.

continued as a threat for much longer than the competitive life-span of most designs.

The first Block Island 40 in competition, Fred Lorentzen's *Seal,* made her debut by winning the 1958 Edlu Trophy on Long Island Sound, and the ten boats built the first year compiled quite a record in their first season. This included wins in the Edgartown Regatta, first in class in the Vineyard Race, fourth overall in the Chicago-Mackinac, 5–6–7 in fleet in the Bermuda Race, and many other similar feats.

Then that winter Ben duPont's *Rhubarb* won the Miami-Nassau Race under demanding conditions after a stirring duel with her sister ship, Jimmy Mullen's *Southern Star,* and those in the sailing world who had not already heard of him really began to be aware of the name Tripp. This started an important association between Tripp and Mullen, and another yachtsman who decided to get on the Tripp wagon for a serious go at racing success was a New York shipping executive named Sumner A. (Huey) Long. He had been campaigning a secondhand German yawl named *Ondine,* and when she was lost on Anegada Reef on a passage to the Caribbean, Long signed up Tripp to follow the success of *Touche* and the BI 40s with a 57-foot aluminum yawl, also to be called *Ondine.* She was built at Jakobson's yard in Oyster Bay, Long Island, with the emphasis first on strength and second on weight-saving in her plating, but she still achieved a lighter weight than a comparable wooden boat. With her wide beam and low center of gravity, she was designed for great sail-carrying ability and passaging performance and became one of the most successful yachts in history in this respect, under an owner eager to campaign her in all the oceans of the world.

She made the starting line of the 1960 Bermuda Race with people still putting her together, but survived the heavy blow that year without incident and then went on to win Class A in the Transatlantic Race to Sweden. In a hyperactive career, she placed on the prize list in over 60 per cent of the contests she entered and garnered many a top trophy. Her wide-ranging campaign made the distinctive Tripp profile a familiar sight in all waters, a "trademark" that appeared in his designs for many years—flared bow, strong sheer, and rather low, almost squat, broad stern, carrying on the look of *Katingo, Touche,* the BI 40, and later designs like the Invicta. *Burgoo,* an Invicta built by Pearson and sailed by Milton Ernstof and a hard-driving crew of Narragansett Bay small-boat sailors, was second in 1962 and first in 1964 in the Bermuda Race, the first fiberglass boat to win that event, and, at 37 feet, the smallest winner in its history. *Ondine* also helped the Tripp image by winning Class A in 1964.

The Block Island 40, of which Swamp Yankee *has been one of the most continuously successful examples, was one of the first designs to demonstrate that a stock fiberglass boat could be a winner in top competition.*

Burgoo, *an Invicta 37, was the first fiberglass boat
ever to win the Bermuda Race, in 1964.*

Left, the 57-foot Ondine, *which made her debut in the 1960
Bermuda Race, probably covered as many miles engaging
in ocean racing as any boat ever has, and her record
was consistently in the prize-winning category.*

In addition to Pearson, other stock builders began to turn to Tripp for designs. For Hinckley he turned out the Bermuda 40, a development on the BI 40, and these boats started to earn prizes in events like the Transpac, Halifax Race, and Transatlantic Race. Hinckley has built well over 100 Bermuda 40s, as they have remained popular as comfortable, beautifully fitted cruising boats following their early racing success.

Another interesting Tripp development was the 42-foot aluminum Raider Class, of which Jack Sutphen's *Scorpion* was the prototype. She was a light displacement design with a developed surface for simplifying construction with flat plates of aluminum, and a tremendous amount of space down below. Ten years after she was built, she still managed to win her class in Block Island Week. She also showed a later Tripp trend, a tendency to higher and higher freeboard to gain space below and, often, to give a good flush-deck platform for racing efficiency. The distinctive touch of a couple of hull portholes also was usually a part of this practice.

One of the most significant affiliations in Tripp's career began in the mid sixties when he designed the first of many boats he went on to turn out for Columbia Yacht Corporation. This was the Columbia 50, at the time the largest production fiberglass sailboat. She made her debut in the 1966 SORC and contained many innovations and developments, rare at the time, that have since become widely accepted. She was semilight displacement, with a separate spade rudder, a high ballast displacement ratio flush deck, split cockpit and great amount of room below decks. The boat caught on well enough to race as a one-design class in California waters, an unusual development for boats that size.

This was the first of many Columbia designs to be widely accepted in cruising and racing circles. The Columbia 57 followed the 50, and *Concerto* took her class in the 1969 Transpac, as well as the La Paz Race that year ahead of a sister ship. The Columbia 43 was an immediate racing success when she came out in 1970, along with a full range of Columbia designs in the 20- and 30-foot categories. Coronado Yachts, like Columbia a Whittaker Corporation subsidiary, has also used many Tripp designs, concentrating on roomy cruising boats as well as some racing designs.

Some of the last boats he did for Columbia and Coronado clearly illustrated Tripp's versatility. A Columbia 30 made for the IOR Mark III was a real "hot" boat with fin keel and beautifully faired underbody, while two other designs showed his increasing attention to all-out cruising boats. Many of his ocean racers had long been noted for their roominess and easy adaptation to comfortable cruising, but the Columbia 45 and Coronado 41 were in the forefront of a new trend

The Hinckley Bermuda 40, originally in the top ranks of ocean racers,
became a classic cruising type, with one of the industry's
longest histories as a production model,
after rule changes eased her out of major competition.

The Columbia 50 combined cruising amenities with racing prowess and introduced many new ideas to stock fiberglass production.

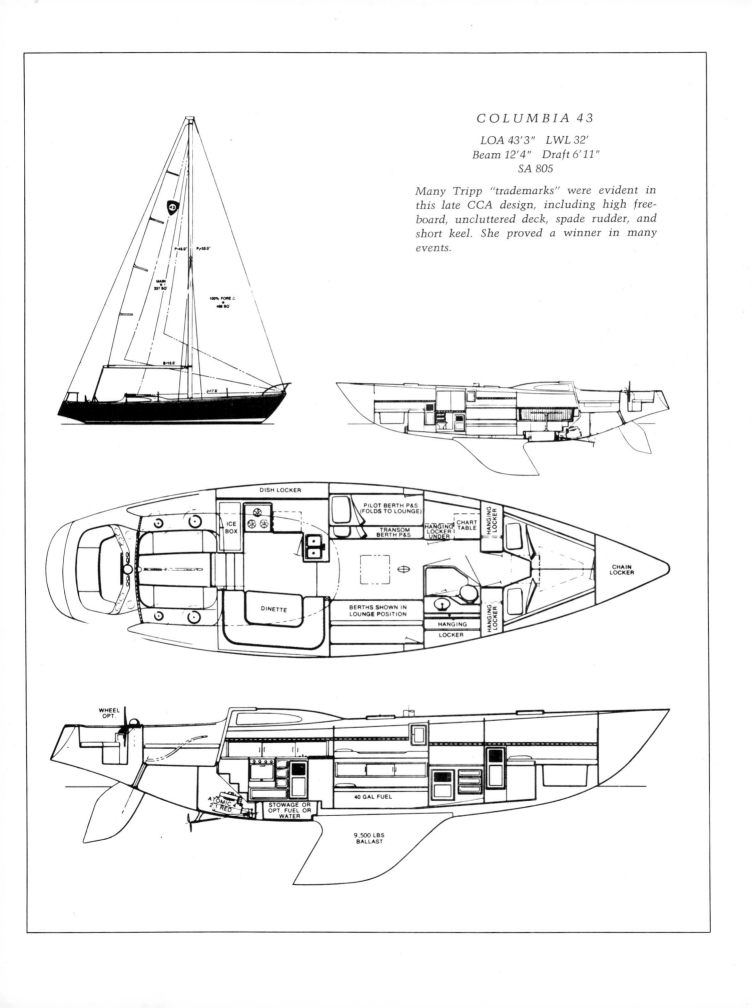

COLUMBIA 43

LOA 43'3" LWL 32'
Beam 12'4" Draft 6'11"
SA 805

Many Tripp "trademarks" were evident in this late CCA design, including high free-board, uncluttered deck, spade rudder, and short keel. She proved a winner in many events.

that developed in the early 1970s. Many powerboat owners were thinking about switching to the more varied challenge of sail, but they did not want to give up powerboat roominess and comfort; these two Tripp boats showed marked ingenuity in combining the requirements in an interesting compromise. Both designs used the underbody of proven racing hulls so that their sailing qualities were assured; in addition, their rigs were efficient, although cut down from ocean-racer proportions, and much easier to handle. In their accommodations, with high freeboard, center cockpits, and roomy after cabins, however, they provided all the amenities of the most comfortable cabin cruiser, with decor to match.

These stock designs kept Tripp busy at his board and his name constantly before the buying public. His reputation was such that his name was prominently used in advertising, but this was not to say he had deserted custom designing by any means. Three whopping big aluminum "superboats" from the Tripp board caused quite a stir in the late sixties. Intrigued more and more with the glamour of first-to-finish and all-out boat-for-boat competition with the top of the fleet, Huey Long gave the 57-foot *Ondine* to the Naval Academy and commissioned his next design by that name to be a maximum 73-footer, ranking right at the top limit of boats allowed in the Bermuda Race. The same design, Tripp Number 220, with many individual variations, was also used by another yachtsman with the first-to-finish bug, Ken DeMeuse of San Francisco, who had kept the big schooner *Serena* going somewhat beyond her expected life-span as a top-of-the-fleet campaigner. His version of Design 220, lighter than *Ondine* and modified in rig, was named *Blackfin.* Between them, these two speedsters rapidly added to the legends of the sport in varied ways. *Ondine* debuted by winning the 1968 Buenos Aires–Rio Race, and *Blackfin* became embroiled in one of the famous sailing controversies of all time when she dueled with *Windward Passage* in the 1969 Transpac. Both these boats broke the old course record—a dramatic battle in which *Passage* was ahead—but because of a two-hour penalty for a starting-line foul, *Passage* was dropped behind *Blackfin* in the record book. Though both had broken the old mark, *Blackfin* held the new one officially until *Passage* again smashed it two years later with *Blackfin* hot on her stern.

In many of the major races, Tripp sailed on boats of his own design as an important member of the afterguard, sometimes as the sailing master, and ranked as a sailor about as high as he did as a designer. His presence aboard often brought a prize to the boat, as he was a tough, experienced campaigner who knew how to get the most out of what he had designed.

The Tripp family is a sailing one, and Tripp's son Bill started well in carrying on the family tradition. He became one of the hot Lightning skippers on

Jolie Madame, *a Mercer 44 stock Tripp design,*
making knots toward Nassau in the SORC

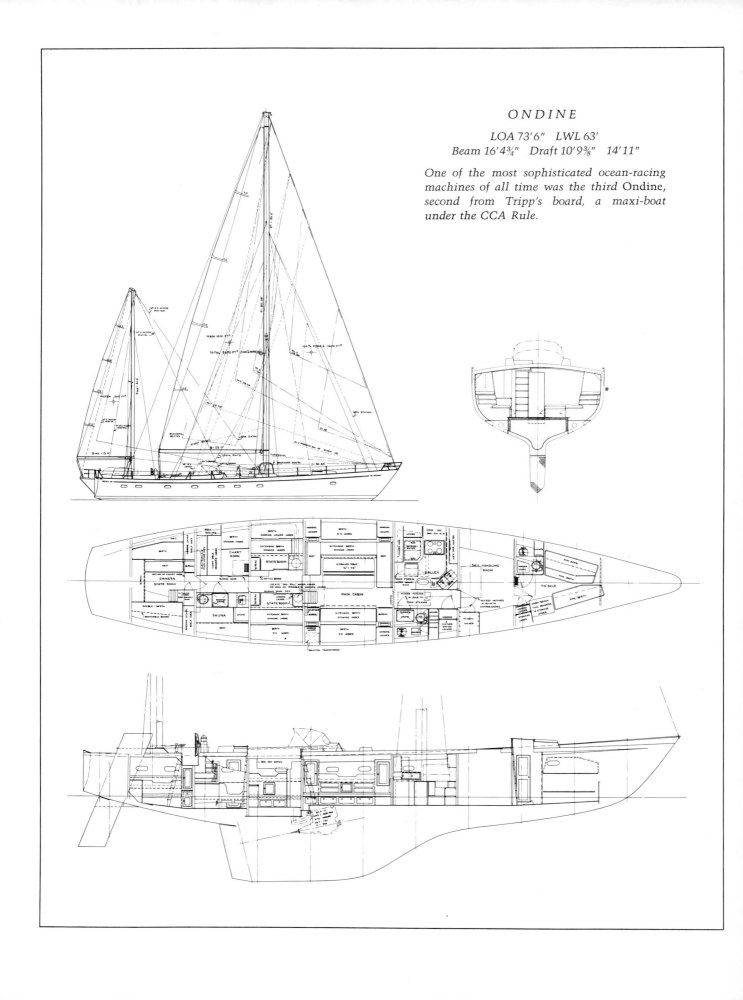

ONDINE

LOA 73'6"   LWL 63'
Beam 16'4¾"   Draft 10'9⅜"   14'11"

One of the most sophisticated ocean-racing
machines of all time was the third Ondine,
second from Tripp's board, a maxi-boat
under the CCA Rule.

The 73-foot Ondine *was one of the last superboats
under the CCA Rule.*

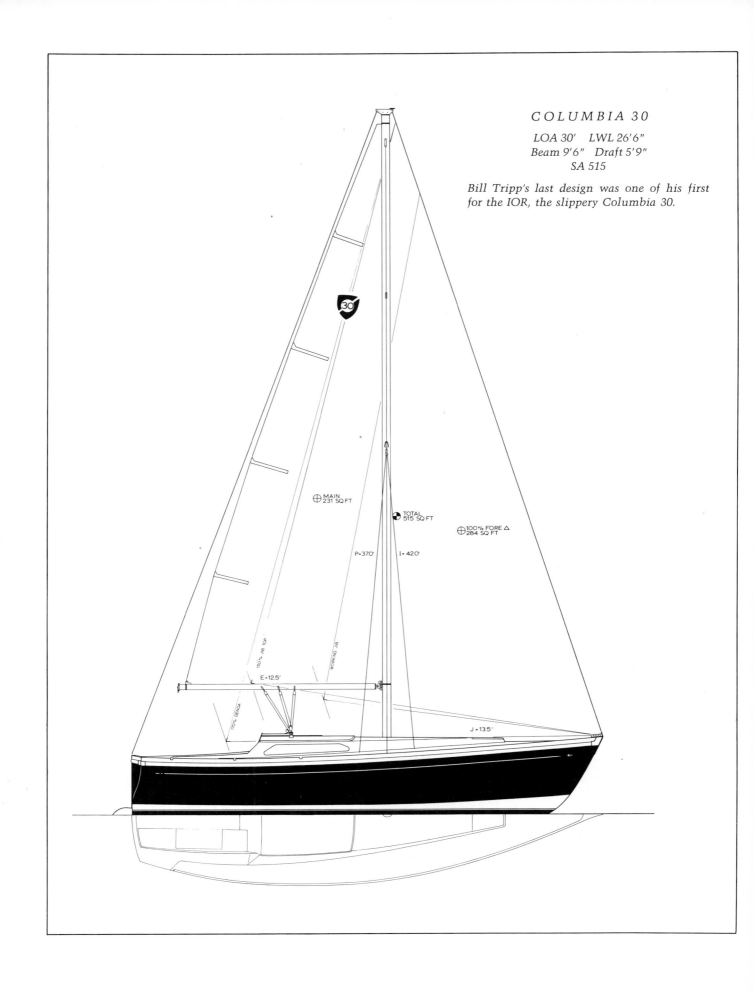

COLUMBIA 30

LOA 30' LWL 26'6"
Beam 9'6" Draft 5'9"
SA 515

Bill Tripp's last design was one of his first
for the IOR, the slippery Columbia 30.

MAIN
231 SQ FT

TOTAL
515 SQ FT

100% FORE △
284 SQ FT

P - 37.0'

I - 42.0'

E - 12.5'

J - 13.5'

150% JIB TOP

WORKING JIB

170% GENOA

Long Island Sound and was a trophy winner for top junior skipper in Manhasset Bay Race Week. Bill Senior tried not to force the issue and to avoid any undue influence or interference, yet a distinct note of pride would creep into his voice when he mentioned his son's success in his typical soft-spoken, slightly diffident manner.

The diffidence and quiet politeness could change to a note of iron, however, if he got on a subject about which he had strong opinions, and he was a tough man to have an argument with if his mind was made up.

There was, for example, the case of a new boat for Jim Mullen, who had not been too active in ocean racing for several years, but returned to the fold in 1970 with the most "super" of the three big Tripp designs, an aluminum sloop carrying on the name *Southern Star*. She was built by Stephens Marine in California and is actually 75 feet overall, though her technical overall length under the Cruising Club Rule, under which she was built, is 73 feet. With a 68-foot waterline, she was the ultimate in a racing machine that could possibly be packed in the CCA top limit.

Her career, however, has been limited by the switch to the IOR, as it was almost impossible to bring her down to the IOR top rating limit of 70 feet. Tripp was not pleased with the switch to IOR, and he fought against it as hard as he could, speaking out in no uncertain terms.

At the time of his death, he had just about resigned himself to working with it, which meant virtually starting over, and the Columbia 30 was his first effort in this direction. So many of the features for which he had become famous—the springy sheer, low freeboard aft, and broad beam carried aft, to name a few—fared badly under the IOR switch. One of his few designs to remain competitive was the One Ton Cupper, the *Hawk*, since she had been designed under the old RORC Rule. His last published design, *Katrinka*, was an IOR adaptation of many of *Touche*'s features, and there was no doubt that the Tripp success story would have carried on for many years, no matter what rule was in effect, if the tragic auto accident hadn't ended his career at its peak.

C. Raymond Hunt

Seven

Ray Hunt

Yacht designers, as we have seen, are divided between those who specialize and become famous for one thing and those who can take on almost any kind of assignment. There are also designers who have been through all possible avenues of education, while others, equally successful, have no formal degree to their names.

An excellent example of the "jack of all trades" and the "natural" rather than the formally scientific approach to designing is a stocky, taciturn New Englander named C. Raymond Hunt. Ruddy of complexion, almost perpetually suntanned, and with a beaming friendly smile when something pleases him, Hunt is probably as good a sailor as any yacht designer has ever been, and he has the look of an old salt about him, at ease in sailing clothes and old sneakers. The scope of his work is as varied as that of anyone who has ever been in the field, though his formal education stopped in prep school. In addition to being a designer, he is a talented and experienced participant in the sport who has been far more active afloat than most of his confrères. From the time that he won the Sears Cup as a fifteen-year-old in 1923 and repeated two years later (something seldom accomplished in this competition), he has been a feared and respected competitor in everything from dinghy sailing to 12-Meters.

Successful as he has been with sailboat designs and as a sailor himself, however, it is probably in the powerboat field that he has made his most widely felt

and influential contributions to boating. The familiar Boston Whaler and the deep-V hull, both products of his lively imagination, are two of the most significant powerboating developments of the twentieth century.

If any one trait could be said to characterize both his work and his performance as a sailor, it would be this ability to feel something instinctively. Even as a youngster, he had a natural touch on the helm that was uncanny. His earliest sailing was among the tidal currents and flats of Duxbury Harbor, south of Boston on Massachusetts Bay, starting in a little Duxbury Duck. He was picked to represent Duxbury Yacht Club in the Sears competition at Marblehead in the junior championship series that had started in 1921. The contest was then for crews from New England and Long Island Sound and had not been expanded into the continent-wide event it has become, but it was the top sailing prize open to juniors at that time.

The 1921 champion was still involved and was heavily favored in the tournament-type eliminations, but Hunt sailed coolly at all times in both light and heavy air, made excellent starts, and held onto the advantage they gave him. At the award ceremony, the chairman said, "I did not see you make a mistake from start to finish."

Along with his touch and his starting ability, Hunt seemed to have a nose for wind shifts and lifts. He won the 1925 championship (after being runner-up in 1924 with President Calvin Coolidge in attendance as a spectator) by picking up a big lift on the last leg of the last race, coming from behind to win by fifty-seven seconds.

He was always noted for his sailing touch, and yet his son Jim, the North American Yacht Racing Union Mallory champion in 1968, remembers how little verbal advice he gathered while sailing with his father as a youngster. "People would go out with Father hoping to pick something up from him, but he couldn't explain things. He did it all by feel and touch. He is also the calmest man I've ever sailed with," Jim has said.

This "natural" approach carried over into Hunt's designing methods. Often the original idea for an important new design would start on the back of an envelope or piece of scratch paper. The concept of *Easterner,* the handsome 12-Meter he designed for the Chandler Hovey family for the 1958 America's Cup trials, came to life on top of a grand piano at his country place in Tilton, New Hampshire.

Hunt switched from Duxbury's shallows, where racing schedules were governed by the state of the tide, to Marblehead, on the other side of Boston, about the time he finished his educational career at Andover (without graduating) and plunged into the heavy competition there. While holding jobs first in the textile

Drumbeat was one of Hunt's better-known and more successful ocean-racing designs.

business and then as a stockbroker, he was sailing in the R Class, then about the most highly competitive one in that hotbed of sailboat racing. One of the R Class's aces was the designer Frank C. Paine, and when Hunt began to beat him with an old and supposedly outdated boat, Paine took notice of the youngster. Eventually he asked Hunt to come to work in his office, and it was there that Hunt picked up his basics, working also with Norman L. Skene, Paine's engineering partner (and author of the standard text *Elements of Yacht Design*). This was top-level guidance for an "apprentice."

Hunt kept up his racing, and Paine had him sail the 8-Meter *Gypsy* (at age twenty-one) in the 1929 Seawanhaka Cup competition. He won the American eliminations with a crew of three in what was supposed to be a five-man boat, but after his selection he was forced by the committee to fill out his crew to five. He lost the match narrowly and has always maintained that the extra two crew members, who didn't fit in with his own slick working small crew, gummed up the works.

Added experience was gained aboard the Paine-designed J boat *Yankee* in the closely fought 1934 America's Cup trials. *Yankee* finally lost by one second to *Rainbow* in the last elimination race. Hunt was a sail trimmer and concerned with tuning, and stood occasional wheel tricks. Tuning was to become another one of his specialties. Hunt could step aboard a boat and make a few effective adjustments by feel—with no concrete explanation of them forthcoming.

By 1938, he felt able to branch out on his own, and his first designs were an interesting combination of the traditional and the unconventional—a foretaste of the versatility he was to show in the years ahead. His first assignment was from Llewellyn Howland of South Dartmouth, Massachusetts, to design a cruising-racing auxiliary to replace a boat that had been lost in the 1938 hurricane. The result was a 39-foot yawl adapted especially to the heavy breezes and steep chop of Buzzards Bay, and the design became the Concordia yawl. As well as being one of the earliest, this proved to be one of the longest-lasting stock auxiliary designs in the history of the sport, with a production life of almost 30 years via the Howland yard, and over 100 boats built to it before changing fashions and construction methods ended its career. For years, Concordias were the "boat to beat" in major events, and Concordia No. 2, Dan Strohmeier's *Malay*, became the smallest boat up to that time to win the Bermuda Race when she topped the fleet in 1954.

The hull had a basic seakindliness that made the Concordia a very comfortable boat in rough water, as well as dry, and fast in a variety of conditions. No matter what convolutions the rating rule went through during the life of the design, Concordias always seemed to rate well and to sail up to their rating, and it really

Malay, *an early Concordia 39, was the smallest boat ever to win
the Bermuda Race when she pulled it off in 1954. This seakindly design
had a long competitive career under the CCA Rule.*

wasn't until the IOR Mark III became established that this very traditional-looking design could really be called out of date. In the 1968 Bermuda Race, Glenn McNary's Concordia, *Westray,* won her class—not bad going for a thirty-year-old design.

The other design of Hunt's from that inaugural year of 1938 was the 110 Class 24-foot one-design racing sloop, and this boat is still going strong as one of the solidest international one-design classes. Hunt made use of plywood, just recently available for marine construction at that time, in the basically simple double-ended design of the 110. Traditionalists howled at her "cigar-box" hull and plumb ends, but she was easy and inexpensive to build and was years ahead of the field in the realm of light, semiplaning boats. This fin-keeler still performs with the most modern hot boats. In her use of plywood and odd boxy lines, she was an early indicator of how Hunt's thinking tended along lines of function, breaking with conventional concepts if necessary, or, as with the Concordia, staying with tradition (though it was unusual to build stock auxiliaries in any number at the time she was conceived) because it fitted in with her intended function.

During the war, Ray had a chance to play with some more unconventional concepts. He had been called from Coast Guard duty to the design section of the Navy Bureau of Ships, where he began to develop plans for a high-speed destroyer. The idea tested well, but there was no time to implement it into a full-sized ship under the rush of wartime crash programs of construction. Instead, Hunt adapted the destroyer lines to a small powerboat in which he went lobstering in his spare time. This personal testing in all kinds of conditions proved helpful later.

Returning to civilian designing after the war, he began to turn out plans for powerboats based on his destroyer and lobster boat experience. Of modified V shape, they were known as Huntforms. His first design, for a 39-foot utility cruiser, appeared in *Yachting* in December 1945.

In the sailboat field, one of his first postwar designs became the 30-foot International 210 sloop, double-ended but otherwise with not quite the same concept as the 110. This class also gained wide acceptance, its popularity partially based on low cost for its size.

Continuing work with high-speed powerboats, by 1950 Hunt had come up with a 42-foot express cruiser for Bradley Noyes of Marblehead that had a top speed of 55 m.p.h., and this ushered him into a period of intense activity and progress in the 1950s. He had, incidentally, played around with a cat-rigged catamaran, and built one over forty feet in 1949, but he didn't continue with multihulls at the time. Only recently has he become interested in them again and has taken on a project for a 70-foot trimaran design.

*The 110 Class sloop, a shocker when she was introduced
just before World War II, has proved to be one of the longest-lived and
most continuously competitive designs in the history of one-design racing.*

Left, adapted to cruiser hulls, the Huntform underbody, with a deep V and longitudinal stringers, brought a new dimension to stock boat performance.

Below, Hunt revolutionized offshore powerboat racing with the Huntform configuration, as dramatized by the succession of Moppies.

HUNT 42

LOA 42'   LWL 38'10"
Beam 14'2"   Draft 3'

This express cruiser was designed to go 55 m.p.h.

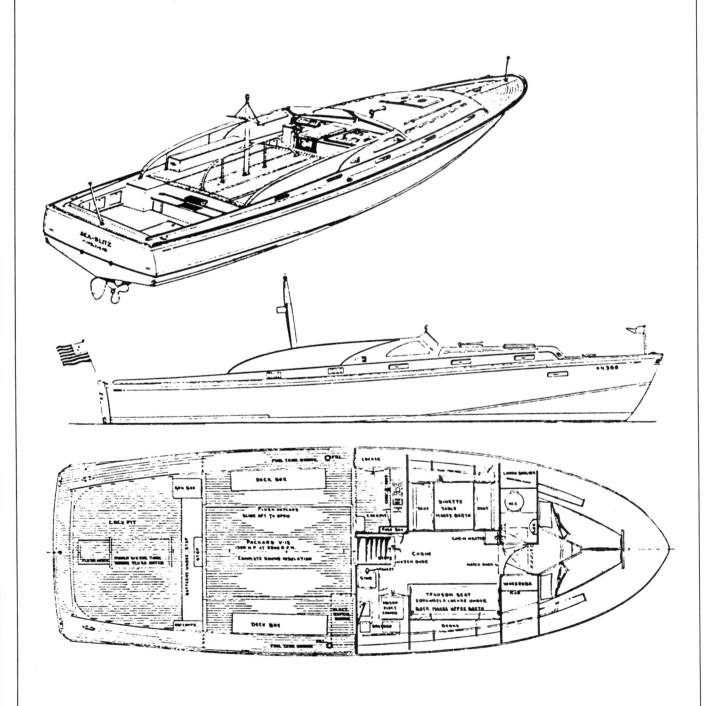

CONCORDIA 41

LOA 41'   LWL 29'6"
Beam 10'3"   Draft 5'10"
SA 780

A development of the Concordia 39, she was a powerful ocean racer.

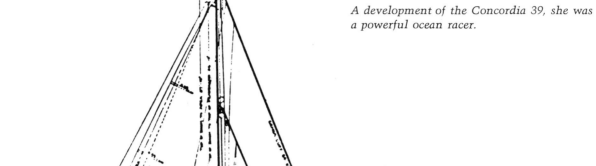

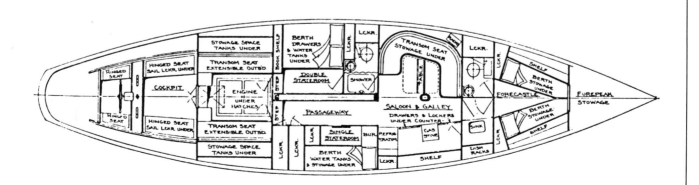

In the ocean-racing field during the fifties, Hunt worked on an enlarged Concordia design, producing a 41-foot sloop version. The first one, *Actaea,* for Commodore Harry Sears of the New York Yacht Club, won the 1955 New London-Annapolis Race. At the same time, Hunt, with his wife and four children, two of them teen-agers, as entire crew, was campaigning *Harrier,* also a 41-foot Concordia, in British waters, shaking up the gathering at Cowes Week with six straight victories. *Harrier* came home to continued success in U.S. events in the next few years and was the instrument for a zany Hunt experiment in the 1959 Annapolis-Newport Race. To dramatize his dislike for genoa jibs, he had her rigged as a giant catboat (just a mainsail with the mast stepped forward), but the experiment was inconclusive—she finished in the middle of the fleet in a fluky race, which Ray felt would have happened with her conventional sloop rig as well. George Hinman's *Sagola,* New York Yacht Club flagship, was another Concordia 41 to build an outstanding record. She received the Cygnet Cup as the top boat on the NYYC cruise in 1962, which *Harrier* had taken in 1957 after also winning the Annapolis-Newport Race that year.

Hunt wasn't able to attend the prize-award ceremony at Newport, as he was already on his way to England for the launching of one of his most interesting ocean racers, Max Aitken's *Drumbeat.* She incorporated some unusual ideas at the time, including a "keelless" underbody which featured an iron casting faired into the double-planked teak construction in place of a timbered keel. A centerboard slot for a very deep board went through the casting. His associate, Fenwick Williams, who did much of the technical work in the Hunt office, was co-credited with this design.

Typical of his versatility, Hunt, while involved with these ocean racers, was also working on other widely varying projects in 1956. One was the Boston Whaler for the Fisher-Pierce Company, a boat that was practically to take over the outboard utility field for a while, and the other had to do with 5.5-Meters and Olympic sailing.

One of the most oft-told tales in sailing history is the story of how the Hunt-designed *Quixotic* failed to gain the 1956 5.5-Meter berth. She was turned out for Ted Hood, then a comparatively unknown young sailor from Marblehead, and she was the sensation of the selection trials on Buzzards Bay. Going into the last race, *Quixotic* had the series wrapped up as long as she beat one boat, and, even if she were last, her closest rival had to win the race to beat her in the series. She had been cleaning up impressively so this seemed like a ridiculous prospect, but the virtually impossible set of circumstances needed to knock her out managed to fall together. Halfway through the race she was near the front of the fleet while

Above, Easterner *had graceful lines and powerful sections that produced a great turn of speed when things were right for her.*

Left, typical of Hunt's ability to poke fun at established rules and concepts was his stunt of rigging the 41-foot Concordia sloop Harrier, *a highly successful ocean racer, as a catboat for the Annapolis-Newport Race in 1959.*

Ray Hunt's Easterner *was an America's Cup contender in 1958
and showed flashes of great speed. As* Newsboy,
her competitive career on the West Coast was a long one.

the boat standing second was in fourth place, and tickets to Australia were practically in the crew's pockets, when the shackle of her main halyard opened. The sail came down, and she staggered in last while the second boat, once the opportunity opened up, moved into first and clinched the berth.

The 1960 Olympic 5.5 selection turned into a happier story for Hunt. A boat of his design, *Minotaur,* seemed to be very fast, but George O'Day managed to win the series in another boat. After the series, O'Day exercised his prerogative to switch boats, took *Minotaur* over, and won the Gold Medal at Naples, with Ray's son Jim in the crew. Hunt himself won the 1963 5.5 World Championship in *Chaje II* by such a convincing margin that he had it sewed up after five of the seven races. Very few other designers have been world champion skippers.

His America's Cup involvement was not quite as successful, although *Easterner* was always conceded to have a potential that had never been fully exploited. She was especially beautiful, with natural topsides, one of the last really "yachty" Cup boats. Although she failed to survive into the final selections the two times she was a defense candidate, she showed flashes of speed and power that were truly impressive.

Under the dictates of the 12-Meter Rule, which establishes certain specifications, Hunt designed her with minimum bow girth penalty, insignificant girth penalty, and comparatively small stern girth penalty. She had no freeboard, draft, or displacement penalties, which therefore allowed her good sail area, ample ballast, and a long waterline. Her ends were nicely balanced and her sheer pleasantly springy. Ray sailed her himself in some of her trials and still had his uncanny knack for picking up a wind shift or new breeze as well as his touch on the helm and mastery of tactics. There was a school of thought that felt she could have realized her potential better if he had sailed her regularly, but she was intended as a family project by the owners.

Sold to the West Coast, renamed *Newsboy,* and slightly altered to take part in offshore races, she has proved a success there. Hunt himself felt that she was a good boat, perhaps even outstanding, and that her America's Cup effort suffered from a lack of the proper sails, administrative problems, and a lack of tuning. "Everything was late," he commented.

That he could have a magic touch on tuning was testified by Carleton Mitchell, who once described Ray coming aboard Mitchell's *Caribbee* in business shirt and tie and quietly making a few suggestions. "He calmed us with his casual manner," Mitchell said, "and I felt I had never steered so well."

To go back from the top of the size scale to the bottom, it was during this period that Hunt's power designs began to make such a name for themselves. The

The Boston Whaler, here shown in the 13½-foot model, was an entirely new concept in outboard motorboat hulls, and its spread has been worldwide.

Fisher-Pierce Company had developed a new sandwich process for fiberglass construction, and Hunt felt that an adaptation of the old sea-sled type might be a good way to make use of it. Doodling on an envelope, he sketched out a flat-bottom skiff and played with a wooden prototype he built himself in one weekend. After tests on the lake near Tilton, he came up with the idea of the center (third) sponson between the two wing sponsons that the sea sled had featured, and the now-familiar Whaler design became a fact. Dick Fisher of Fisher-Pierce refined it some and began to build and promote it, adding a 16-footer of Hunt's design a few years later, and the result was one of the most popular and widely used designs in pleasure-boating history.

As an outgrowth of his early lobster-boat and destroyer experiments, and the steady building of Huntform powerboats, he had refined his concept to a deep-V design that was used in a utility tender during the America's Cup trials in 1958. Dick Bertram, who had been building up a Florida yacht brokerage business while still active as a top racing sailor, was impressed with the speed, seakeeping ability, and dryness of the little boat, which he saw zipping around the anchorage at Newport while he was crewing on *Vim*. He thought it would be just the design for a boat that could do well in the rugged Miami-Nassau powerboat race, and he ordered the 30-foot *Moppie* from Hunt's designs for the 1960 race. She ran away with it in very rough conditions, starting a string of unprecedented wins in offshore powerboat racing.

In this unique development of the V-bottom form, the V is carried aft with only moderate loss of deadrise; fore-and-aft strakes, or lift chines, give extra lift and spray deflection; and the hull planes with very little change of trim. It "squishes" into head seas, rather than pounding, and even at top speed has great roll and directional stability.

The achievement of *Moppie* and her successors led to the establishment of Bertram Yacht Corporation for the production of stock fiberglass cruisers of the same design. The original *Moppie* was used as a plug for the boat that became the Bertram 31, and in a ten-year period well over 1000 of these boats were turned out. When Dick Bertram sold out and started another firm for the importation of premium luxury yachts built in Japan, he once again turned to Ray Hunt for the deep-V design of the 56- and 63-footers that carried the same performance qualities into a much larger-sized hull than ever before. Custom designs, such as Tom Sopwith's 75-foot *Philante V* built in England by Camper and Nicholsons in 1961, were forerunners of this work.

It is a measure of Hunt's originality that the Boston Whaler design has been copied, adapted, and modified in hundreds of versions by other designers and

BERTRAM 38

LOA 37'9"   LWL 35'
Beam 14'6"   Draft 3'5"

The Huntform hull concept was adapted into
this comfortable and luxurious stock cruiser.

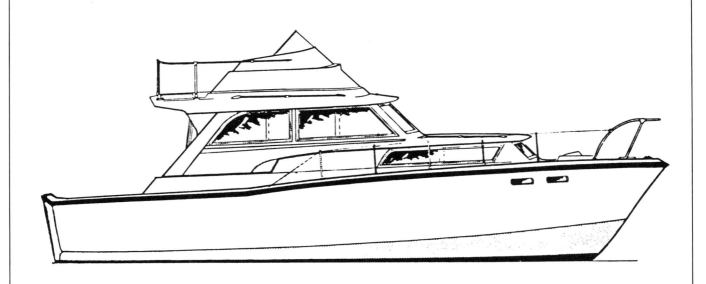

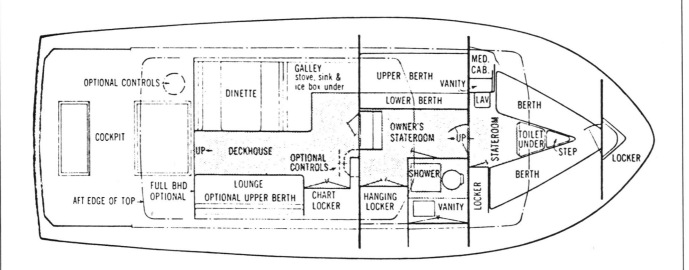

builders once his original showed the way to the performance qualities of the type. The fantastic stability and the ease with which the hull can be driven by comparatively low power were a revelation in a field that most people thought had been completely covered. His deep-V design was also extensively adapted and copied after its worth had been proven. No one thought a boat could go as fast in rough water as this design did until the advent of *Moppie* and her sisters. "You had to have a flat-bottom planing hull to go fast and it pounded too much to operate in rough water" was the way the thinking went before Hunt's theories became reality.

It is unusual that these ideas came from a man with no formal training, and it is equally surprising that such a seakindly hull as the Concordia and such a radical innovation as the inexpensively built 110 were also the products of one man. Put all these boats side by side and no one would think to identify them as the work of one design board, but Ray Hunt was always doing what came naturally and all these designs were based on natural function.

C. William Lapworth

Eight

Bill Lapworth

In February 1964, in the comparative infancy of stock fiberglass boats as ocean racers, a short-ended sloop of moderately light displacement came out of California to take the Southern Ocean Racing Conference championship. Named *Conquistador,* she was No. 2 of a stock line known as the Cal-40, and, starting with that highly prized and well-publicized title, an unprecedented string of victories in major ocean-racing events was chalked up by this design. The effect on the whole sport was profound, giving impetus to a "revolution" that is still going on, and it also propelled the designer C. William Lapworth into front rank prominence among the naval architects in yachting.

Not that Bill Lapworth, a forty-four-year-old transplanted Michigan native, was unknown at the time. Especially in California, he had achieved local stature as an advocate of light displacement. The L-36 Class had become the biggest class of one-design ocean racers up to that time with over seventy boats, and his unusual-looking reverse-sheer design, *Nalu II,* had won the 1959 Transpac. In 1963, the Cal-24, the first boat from his board for the new firm of Jensen Marine, had won her division in *Yachting's* One-of-a-Kind Regatta, followed by the Cal-20, also a new Jensen model, for a Lapworth sweep.

These successes and others had gained him growing attention among those who keep an eye on likely prospects, but it was the Cal-40, which Jensen brought

out in the fall of 1963, that sent his name across the yachting firmament like a skyrocket. *Conquistador* lit the fuse, and the design took off from there with three successive Transpac victories starting in 1965, the 1966 SORC, and the 1966 Bermuda Race. This still stands as the most remarkable record of victory in major races for a stock design, and there were, of course, wins in a host of other events.

It got to the point where, after the Bermuda Race in 1966, a frustrated participant was passing cards out to the group on the lawn of the Royal Bermuda Yacht Club bearing the message that they were for membership in the "Help Stamp Out Cal-40s Association, C. William Lapworth, Pres." The design had taken five out of the first fifteen in fleet, four in the first nine, and was one, three, four, five, six in Class D. To add to this dominance, a Cal-36, Lapworth's next smallest version incorporating the principles of the Cal-40, was seventh in fleet and second in Class E.

The Cal-40's special features and general characteristics provide a distillation of much that Lapworth had been practicing since the early fifties, and the design philosophy he has always worked by was well embodied by it. Typically, he has gone for speed and performance with little regard for rating under the rule. Most Cal-40s hit about 31.6 under the version of the CCA rule then in use, rather high for a boat with a 30½-foot waterline, but they sailed up to their rating in almost all conditions. On a clean-lined, moderately light displacement hull, possessing almost the simplicity of a canoe in an arced bottom with hard bilges and flat deadrise, she had a fin keel and spade rudder. Another feature unusual at the time was inboard shroud terminals for better trimming of headsails. They were seated on a transverse bulkhead reinforced with extra strapping. Her accommodations provided quarter berths running the whole length of the cockpit for an uncluttered layout ideal for racing and roomy for cruising.

About the only "weaknesses" in the Cal-40 were an excess of wetted surface in relation to power and slightly full bows, a handicap at wind strengths of about four to ten knots, especially in a slop of sea. In extremely light air, the easily driven hull moved nicely, and above ten knots, the inherent power in the design brought her back to optimum performance. In downwind sailing in heavy air, her surfing ability was a revelation to ocean-racing sailors unused to breaking the "hull speed barrier."

The Cal-40 was a breakthrough for Lapworth in personal prestige, and it set Jensen Marine up as a major factor in the field of building auxiliaries. Until then, very few mass-produced stock boats were serious contenders in ocean racing. Most were aimed at the cruising market, and fiberglass had not been completely ac-

Cal-40s introduced surfing to ocean racing as an accepted phenomenon and provided new excitement never before imagined. Here Melee *surfs into Nassau in a wild welter of spray at the finish of the windblown 1969 Miami-Nassau Race.*

cepted, especially by offshore sailors. Here, however, was a boat that could be put in the water (at that time) for under $40,000 as a serious racing contender, cleaning up against $100,000 custom boats. It was enough to reverse the thinking of a whole sport and to start a strong trend to stock boats as top contenders. A side result was to foster one-design class racing in large auxiliaries, something that had not been done much before.

Perhaps the biggest eye-opener of all, however, was how the design exceeded all previous conceptions of what speeds a boat that size could attain and maintain at sea. A 40-foot boat surfing along for hours on end at 14 to 16 knots, with wings of water arcing out from her hull like a water-skier's wake, was mind-boggling to traditionalists, and virtually a new breed of sailors was created by this type of sailing. Young athletic crews who could stand the constant tension and exhilaration of rides like this drove Cal-40s as ocean racers had never been driven before, and the Transpac was their special place to shine, with its days of downwind surfing.

True, the ride to windward in a sea in these boats was not the smoothest or most seakindly feeling afloat, but performance was still there, and Lapworth had dramatized for a wide public just what this basically simple hull form could do.

Lapworth's is far from a one-boat success story, however. Many other designs, some applying the same principles to different lengths, others putting other considerations into effect, have kept his name on top ever since the Cal-40. The Cal-36 never quite hit the phenomenal record of the Cal-40s, but it too had many successes; the Cal-24 had a long run of dominance in that size range; and the Cal-20 continues as a very popular racing-cruising boat in the minimum size and price category. The Cal-25, Cal-28, Cal-30 and 2-30, Cal-27, Cal-34, Cal-29, Cal-39, Cal 3-30, and Cal-33 have all been the boat to beat in their field as soon as they appeared—thus emphasizing the ability of stock-production boats.

A Cal-20 even made a transatlantic passage after being specially equipped. A prototype of the Cal Cruising 46, Hale Field's *Fram*, embodying able sailing characteristics with motorsailer cruising comfort, made a circumnavigation of North America (with the help of a train ride from Michigan to the Pacific Northwest). The Cal-48 and 43 have combined racing success with cruising comfort.

The 1970 Mazatlan Race was as impressive a Lapworth sweep as the 1966 Bermuda Race. In it, Cal boats took the first three places overall, seven out of the first ten, first in all four classes, second in three, and third in two, for nine out of twelve class places.

The 2-24 was the first of what Lapworth calls the finer-bow models, followed shortly by the 2-30 and the 29, which became a particular terror in light

Lapworth and Jensen Marine combined in a series of stock fiberglass ocean racers, setting a trend in the industry. This is the Cal-34.

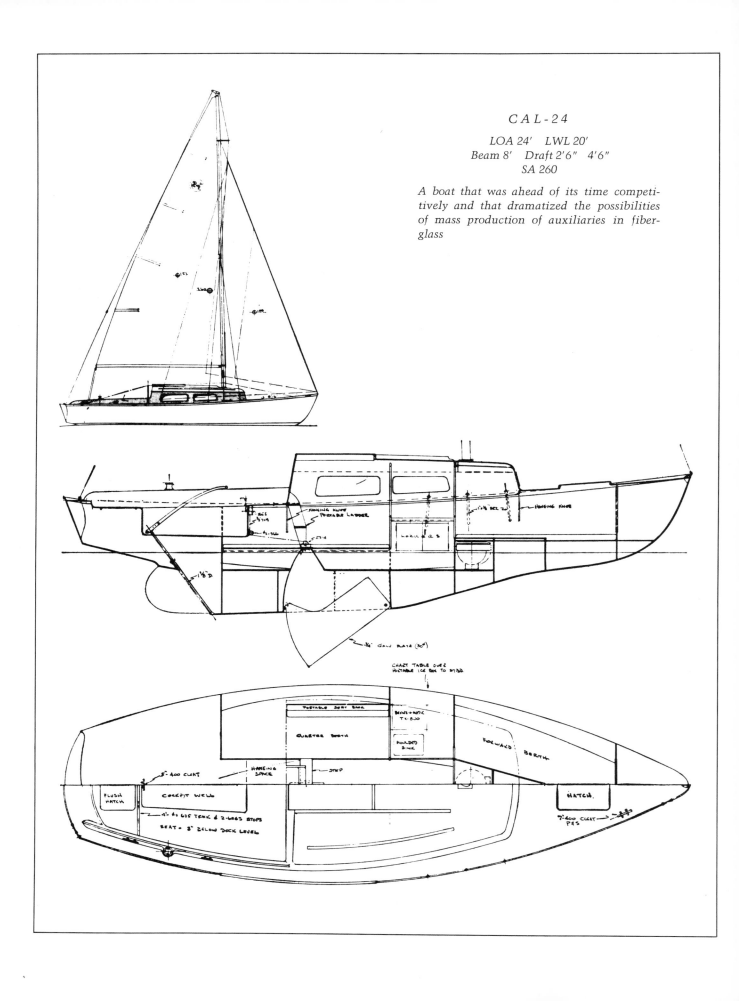

C A L - 2 4

LOA 24'   LWL 20'
Beam 8'   Draft 2'6" 4'6"
SA 260

A boat that was ahead of its time competitively and that dramatized the possibilities of mass production of auxiliaries in fiberglass

The Cal-20 (foreground) developed into the largest one-design class of small ocean racers and has had a longer production life than any other boat in this category.

The Cal-25 pioneered in dramatizing that cruising comfort and a roomy layout could be combined with racing success.

The reverse sheer Nalu II *was a consistent prize winner
in the Transpac, winning Class C four times.*

air. The Cal-34 had been the last of the Cal boats with very full bows. These always did well off the wind and to weather in a breeze, but they were somewhat at a disadvantage to weather in a small chop. In addition to finer bows, the newer boats had shorter keels to reduce wetted surface, and the spade rudder was abandoned for a skeg and spade combination. The Cal 2-30 did particularly well in the 1969 SORC and the New York Yacht Club cruise.

These designs have come from a board in a quiet, moderately cluttered office on a side street in Newport Beach, California. It is in a small, modern office building, where Lapworth works alone, without benefit of secretary and often with the phone turned off if he is concentrating. Recently he has taken to using a small computer for some of his calculating. He lives across the harbor on the mainland side in a Cape Cod-style cottage at the bay's edge. Bill and his second wife, Peg, have remodeled it extensively, and its flower-bedecked terrace looks south over the bustling bay to Newport Harbor Yacht Club and the harbor entrance beyond. The Lapworths love to sit there and watch the passing parade, though Bill will occasionally emit a small, derisive snort if a boat from someone else's design hovers too long in his view.

Slender, quiet and soft-spoken, with a ready smile on his aquiline features, he isn't one to make loud, rude noises about designs he doesn't approve of, and his approach to the subject of boat design is deceptively mild and disarming. Not very often a soapbox orator, he can still become well warmed up when a subject on which he has strong convictions comes under discussion. And he does have strong convictions. For example, he was adamantly opposed to the switch from the CCA Rule to IOR because he didn't think there was a need for such drastic action.

A small, low-speed launch and a new Cal 3-30 are at the pier in front of the house. The Lapworths enjoy jaunts around Newport Harbor in the launch, from which they can check on other boats and developments along the teeming shoreline. When his four children by an earlier marriage, who live nearby, come over, the family often goes sailing, and skiing is another sport they all enjoy very much. Asked if he skis, Bill usually answers, "Not as much as I'd like to."

He does some local racing, although he says he is not a "yacht club type," and is usually found on one of his own designs in the major events. When the Cal-24 won the 1963 One-of-a-Kind cruising division, he was at the tiller with builder Jack Jensen in the crew. In 1964 he was aboard *Conquistador* when she won the SORC and did much of the helming, and he was part of an all-star crew that brought *Thunderbird* first place in the 1966 Bermuda Race. He is quietly efficient aboard a boat, seldom raising his voice; a young schoolgirl, a stranger to him before she crewed for him in a Cal-25 in the 1966 One-of-a-Kind, when

Tampa Bay's breezes were light, baffling and frustrating, said that "he has the patience of a saint."

Bill Lapworth's sailing goes back to boyhood days on the Detroit River, when he started racing Detroit Yacht Club catboats at the age of twelve. He soon moved on to bigger boats, and during college days at Michigan, where he studied naval architecture, he crewed in 6-Meters and in long-distance races such as the Mackinacs. Right after graduation in 1941, he went on navy duty with the Bureau of Ships at Quincy, Massachusetts, and eventually was transferred to San Diego. After the war he decided to remain a Californian and went to work in the naval architect's office of Merle Davis in Los Angeles. Davis died soon afterward, and Lapworth's shingle went up solo.

At the time he was sailing an International 14 dinghy, and developing a preoccupation with light displacement as a result, and this influence showed in one of his first commissions, the light-displacement sloop *Flying Scotchman* for Dick Stewart and Porter Sinclair. She was the first Lapworth boat to make the Design Section of *Yachting,* appearing in February 1950; the commentary treated her as a radical departure, noting her obvious relationship to an International 14. She was 32½ feet overall, 28 feet on the waterline with a fin keel, flat-bottom sections and hard bilge, and she had a displacement of only 6600 pounds. Her construction was cedar-strip planking and canvased plywood decks, her accommodations were very simple, and most of her joinerwork doubled as structural members. Lapworth admits that cost was as much a consideration as performance in hitting on light displacement for this early design, because cost is related to weight in boat construction.

Flying Scotchman was one of seven light-displacement boats entered in the 1950 Bermuda Race, much to the consternation of East Coast traditionalists. There was great advance speculation that she, *Dirigo,* a blown-up Raven, Laurent Giles's *Gulvain,* and a couple of other light little British boats would make all the conventional cruising-boat types in the fleet obsolete.

The *Scotchman,* which had to have a three-foot bustle added on her stern to qualify for the race, did the best of the seven light boats by taking sixth in her class, but none of them set the world on fire. All the prize-winners were conventional "cruising houseboats," as one account put it.

None of the light boats had had a chance to surf during the race, which had fluky, inconclusive conditions, and not many of the crew members ever expected to surf in offshore conditions. *Scotchman* was deemed to have the most comfortable motion. There was general agreement that no light-displacement revolution was

Flying Scotchman *caused a stir as a forerunner of the light-displacement trend.*

imminent, but at least the talk had started. And Lapworth did not give up on his ideas.

Scotchman had done well in West Coast events, however, and Lapworth persisted in his interest in the type. In 1954 the first two boats of the light-displacement L-36 Class came out—George Griffin's *Cassandra* and Bob Allan's *Holiday*—and they immediately started to clean up in Southern California. By the early sixties, seventy-one had been built and they continued to do well until the fiberglass revolution and the continued advance in light-displacement design took over. Several other L classes—24, 40, and 50—came out during the fifties. It was an L-24, *Dove,* that Lee Graham used for most of his voyage as the youngest sailor ever to make a circumnavigation.

It was in 1958 that Lapworth and Jensen hooked up in one of the most significant associations in boating history. Jensen had an engineering background but no professional boatbuilding experience, and he had a notion that production-line construction of small fiberglass auxiliaries would work. Hardly anyone was in the field at the time, and they started out with the Cal-24, which was an immediate success. It was followed by the Cal-20, which has remained in production and now numbers over 1700 boats registered in the class organization of thirty fleets.

Every Jensen boat has been designed by Lapworth, who spends most of his time on these designs but has far from given up custom work. Examples of this include the 48-foot aluminum ketch *Aranji,* which won the 1968 Tahiti Race and has done well in the San Francisco Perpetual Cup; and *Nalu IV,* which made her debut in 1970. In addition to *Fram,* the 43-foot full-powered auxiliary, *Evian,* a wooden sloop, cruised from California to Ireland and back in 1969–70. It was also during this period that the Cal-36 *Agisymba* was sailed by Nancy and John Hutchinson from California to Europe and back to Florida, garnering a class third in the Transatlantic Race to Ireland on the way as well as first in the Around Grenada Race in 1970.

Although most of the emphasis has been on the racing accomplishments of Lapworth designs, and his widest influence has been due to the startling success of the Cal-40 and her sisters, Lapworth boats have always been well adapted to cruising as well as racing. He has often said that "boats are designed for people," and even his smallest ones have always had good roomy bunks and some method of solving the headroom problem. The Cal-25 had an ingenious folding hatch that could be popped up to make full headroom over the galley. Even a "machine" like the Cal-40 had a great deal of bunk space and a spacious layout; and the

The L-36 was one of the first large classes of stock
one-design ocean racers, well in advance of a trend
and also a pacesetter in the light-displacement field.

The Cal-40 was the single most successful stock one-design in ocean-racing history and established stock boats as contenders in the very best competition.

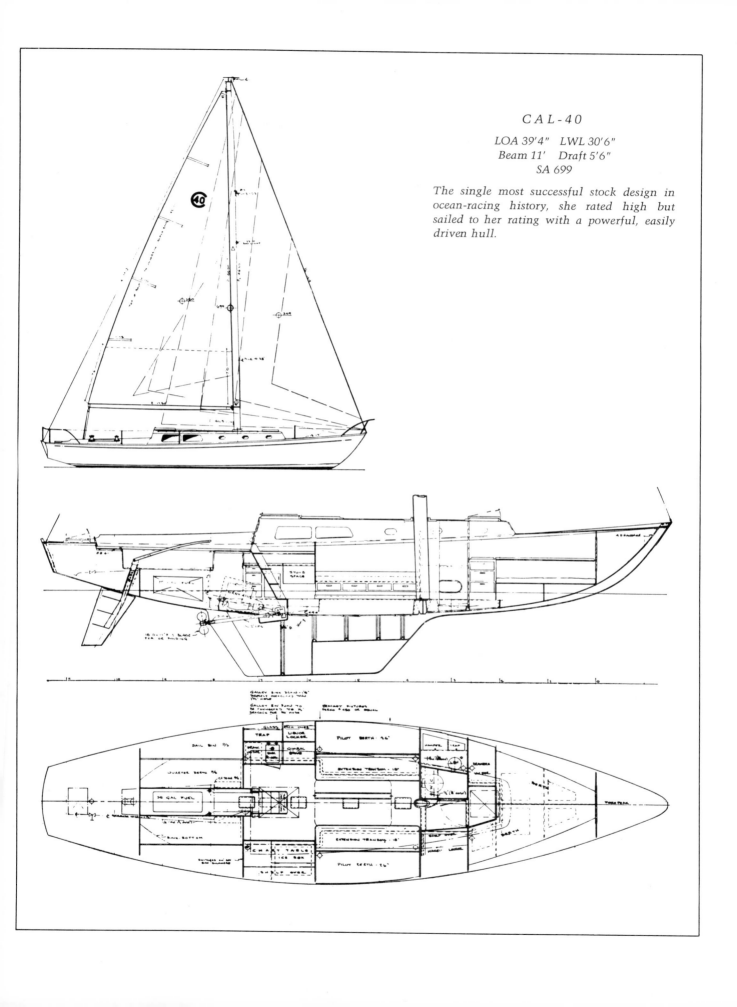

CAL-40

LOA 39'4" LWL 30'6"
Beam 11' Draft 5'6"
SA 699

The single most successful stock design in ocean-racing history, she rated high but sailed to her rating with a powerful, easily driven hull.

CAL 2-46

LOA 45'6"   LWL 37'6"
Beam 12'6"   Draft 5'
SA 784

*A luxurious cruising yacht combining com-
fort with ability under sail and an extra
amount of room for her size*

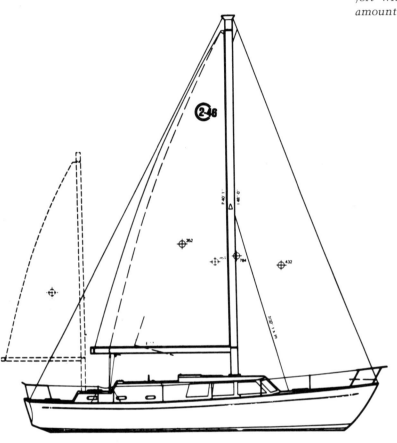

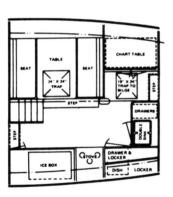

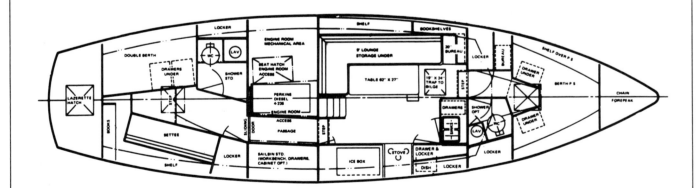

Hutchinsons reported that their two-year voyage in *Agisymba* proved her tremendously comfortable and able as a cruising and passage boat. The Cal Cruising 46 was one of the first "full cruising" boats on the market, based on the custom-designed *Fram*. A later development, the Cal Cruising 2-46, carried this popular trend further, with an ingenious use of space that provided exceptionally roomy accommodations without a bulky look, while retaining good sailing qualities.

In almost every era, certain yacht designers and their ideas have had a profound influence on the sport, in contrast to eminently successful designers whose creations have not brought about such pronounced change. Bill Lapworth is one whose contributions have had a wide effect. In an age when construction methods and racing techniques were advancing more rapidly and radically than they ever had before, his designs of the late fifties and mid sixties created a splash from which the ripples are still spreading. Now that he has achieved top stature in one of the world's most limited and thinly populated professions, his influence will continue to be felt for many years to come.

Olin Stephens

Nine

Olin Stephens

It is an amazing phenomenon, and another indication of how rare real talent, beyond mere competency, has been in the lonely profession of designing yachts, that almost the entire history of the field has been spanned, and can virtually be summed up, by the overlapping careers of two men.

In a collection of greats, Nathanael Herreshoff and Olin Stephens II have to be ranked as the greatest. Herreshoff began his career in the 1860s, Olin Stephens in 1928, when Herreshoff's long one was in its twilight years, and in the 1970s the quiet, professorial New Yorker is unquestionably the dean of the profession. In the sheer number of outstanding boats that have come from his board, he is the single most successful man in the history of the field. Herreshoff's talents were more varied. He was an inventor and an engineer who left his mark on many diverse types of sail and power vessels, and on a great amount of equipment and machinery. The Stephens talent has been directed more single-mindedly to turning out yacht designs that have, of course, covered a wide range of boat types.

With the growth of the sport, his name and the name of his firm, Sparkman and Stephens—with his brother Roderick Jr. as an integral part of the operation—have become known everywhere in the world that boats are sailed. No other designer has had more of his products win trophies, from midget regattas to the America's Cup, and no one has ever had such a profound influence on the sport over such a long period of time that encompassed so many changes and developments. He is truly a "household word" in the sport, and the major success story in it.

There is always the human side of a success story, and the Stephens story is one of quiet dedication to work, with a minimum of flamboyance. What flamboyance there has been has been provided mostly by the vigorous, square-jawed Rod, who is more outgoing and talkative than his older brother, and more of a physical person. When Rod is in a boat, there is no hiding the fact. Quick and agile, he is all over the deck and up the rigging, tuning, adjusting, and covering a host of details with rapid efficiency. A great helmsman and a great "second pair of eyes" to the skipper when it is not Rod's boat, he is the perfect complement, in knowledge, capabilities, and energetic drive, to Olin's more contemplative contributions.

Olin's personality is self-effacing and downright shy. Of medium build, with a smooth face that has remained almost boyish into his sixties, a soft way of talking, and a deliberate, cool manner in approaching any situation, he does not make himself immediately and dramatically evident. If he is in the afterguard of a boat—and he has not sailed a boat of his own in competition since the 1930s— it is not particularly obvious at first glance; but his on-board contributions to the success of his boats have been many and varied over the years. Like his brother he too is invaluable as "second eyes," and his touch on the helm is sure and skillful.

Olin's shyness disappears when he warms up to his subject and his listener, and he is a lucid, easy-to-follow instructor while explaining some theory of design or new idea that he is working on. Without talking down, he can make an abstruse subject amply clear in layman's terms.

Over the years he has worked on many committees developing measurement rules for handicapping, and his talk here, with a group of experts, can be forceful and to the point. His has been the single greatest influence on various rule changes and developments, culminating in the adoption of an International Offshore Rule in the early seventies, though his hours of hard work and dedication were little known outside a small circle of officials. Because he has had so much influence on the establishment of rating rules, and on their provisions, other designers have sometimes resented his position on the "inside track," but the fact remains that the work was done in the face of considerable difficulties and after interminable hours of study and attendance at meetings.

Sparkman and Stephens has become such a familiar part of the sport that it is sometimes hard for modern yachtsmen to envision a time when the name Olin

Edlu II was one of the boats demonstrating characteristics that were developed by Stephens in the 1930s.

Stephens meant nothing in the world of yachting. Every career has to start somewhere, and Olin's first work appeared publicly in the Design Section of the January 1928 issue of *Yachting*. This was for a 6-Meter, and forty-five years and some 225 designs later his work was still a major feature of those pages. *Yachting's* inclusions were of course but a fraction of Olin's total output (which numbers over 2000 designs); nonetheless, they represent by far the largest number of designs from any one man to appear in that section.

There was something a bit prophetic in the editorial comment that went with the plans in 1928. Referring to a recent international 6-Meter series in which the U.S. had not done well, the statement went on: ". . . most of the critics agreed on at least two things, i.e.: American designers had been left far in the rear by their foreign contemporaries, and 'something should be done about it,'" and continued, ". . . at least, the ideas of young designers should see the light of day in the hopes that they might succeed where more experienced naval architects have progressed but little in the past year or so."

Young he definitely was, in fact nineteen, and his formal education in yacht design at the time consisted of little more than a term at M.I.T. in the academic year 1926/27. An attack of jaundice had forced him to leave college before the end of freshman year, and he decided that he would rather get right to the designing of boats instead of studying more about it and therefore never went back. M.I.T. is still proud of him, however, and has put him on its Board of Visitors. In addition, he has earned honorary degrees from Brown University and Stevens Tech, in Hoboken, New Jersey, site of the towing tank that has played such an important part in Stephens' career.

There was also something familiar and prophetic in the designer's comment accompanying the 6-Meter plans.

The design is intended primarily for light weather. In any design the most important factors of speed seem to be long sailing lines and large sail area, with moderate displacement and small wetted surface. Then comes beauty, by which is meant clean, fair, pleasing lines. Though *per se* beauty is not a factor of speed, the easiest boats to look at seem the easiest to drive.

To produce long sailing lines there are two methods available. First by using a long water line coupled with fine ends; second, a shorter water line and full ends. The former method has been used in this design. The water line is about the longest of any existing American "Six." Though this long water line would ordinarily result in small sail area, this has been avoided by reducing the girth and girth difference measurements to the very minimum, which also lessens the wetted surface. The measured sail area is good, while, with overlapping jibs of various sizes, it may be said to be ample for the lightest of weather.

The magazine's commentary then concluded by saying that "this design shows a great deal of promise," an oft-used cliché that couldn't, for once, have been more to the point.

It is also interesting that the facing page in that design section carried a "husky ketch" by John G. Alden, putting two of the most important influences on twentieth-century yachting side by side—at the peak of one career and at the beginning of the other, and with boats that typified their lifetime thinking.

Olin's preoccupation with clean lines, low wetted surface, and an easily driven hull has been a hallmark of his entire career right from this first statement. By the time he got to working on such 12-Meters as *Intrepid,* his concern with beauty might have altered somewhat, but the boats he has turned out all could be said to follow, in general, the principles laid down in that early quote. Of the thousands of designs turned out by Olin and by other designers working under his supervision and the Sparkman and Stephens imprimatur, a large percentage have had outstanding racing success and a tremendous number stand out as boats that have made yachting history.

Dorade was the first, the 52-foot yawl that startled everyone by walking away with the 1931 Transatlantic Race. She was designed when Olin was twenty-one and had only a few formal designs to his credit. Following her, *Stormy Weather, Edlu,* the New York Yacht Club 32 Class, *Blitzen, Baruna, Gesture,* the Pilot Class, *Bolero, Dyna, Finisterre, Venturer, Bay Bea,* and *Noryema* are just a few of the yachts (or types) that have become legends in ocean racing, not to mention such one-design classes as the Blue Jay and Lightning, and Olin's involvement with the America's Cup from the 1937 campaign on. If there was any idea that the "dean" might have lost ground to the onslaught of new talent, the 1972 Bermuda Race was a dramatic refutation. In it, S&S boats compiled their best record since their first class prize, *Dorade's* Class B win in 1932. *Noryema* won it, three other class winners were by S&S, as was second in fleet, and, in all, sixteen S&S designs were on the prize roster, the best performance ever by a single design firm.

To go back to the beginning, how did all this happen? There was no special seafaring tradition in the family as Olin and Rod were growing up in the Mott Haven section of New York City's Bronx, and later in Scarsdale, the Westchester County suburb where both still live. Their father, Roderick Sr., was in the coal business, and the family's first involvement with things nautical came while summering at Cape Cod in 1920.

The Lightning, since its introduction in 1939,
has been one of the most successful one-design classes in history.

Blue Jays proliferated by the thousands as junior trainers.

The family acquired a 16-foot day-sailer named *Corker* in which the boys and their father learned to sail "while doing." Despite a few misadventures, like running aground and having to slog home for miles across the flats, they became entranced with the sport, and they settled early into the approach to it that was to determine how each brother worked out his career. Olin, quiet, unruffled, analytical of mind, was best at the tiller and in directing overall operations, while Rod Jr. was the hyperactive crew.

A succession of family boats on the Cape and later on Long Island Sound out of American Yacht Club, Rye, New York, got them deeply involved with cruising and racing, and boats became virtually an obsession. At Scarsdale High School, where Olin graduated in the class of 1926, his books were covered with doodles and drawings that all turned out to be hull designs, and the best college choice for him seemed the naval architecture department at M.I.T.

When the illness-enforced absence cut short his freshman year there, the chance to proceed directly to designing seemed much more important to the young man with a head bursting with design ideas than a return to the dry theory of the classroom. As a result he became one of the better arguments for "dropping out." Rod became another one when he tried Cornell for a year but decided he felt much more at home in the boatbuilding trade on City Island. After a summer job there, he decided to stay on and not go back to college either.

Bowing to this obvious drive toward involvement with boats, the senior Stephens arranged a meeting between Olin and a youthful yacht broker named Drake Sparkman, who was looking for a designer so that he could expand his firm to include naval architecture as well as brokerage. Although Olin was not yet twenty, Sparkman, mainly on a hunch after studying the plans Olin had already produced, and being impressed by his quiet confidence, offered him a partnership on an informal basis that would become a formal one if things were going well when Olin turned twenty-one on April 13, 1929.

Early commissions didn't pour in. The first one was to design a 21-foot training boat for the Junior YRA of Long Island Sound, and Sparkman persuaded a friend of his, Arthur Hatch, to use a design of Olin's for a new 30-foot ocean-racing sloop, *Kalmia*. With Olin as skipper, she won her class in the 1929 race from New London to Gibson Island, Maryland (beating the well-known yachting journalist Alf Loomis in *Hotspur*, among others, with the famous schooner *Nina* taking the fleet prize), a long-drawn-out light-weather affair that tried the patience of the crews in the little boats as they worked up the Chesapeake.

This was an encouraging start, but it took a customer with a special interest

The New York 32 popularized the stock ocean racer concept far ahead of its day. Olin's brother Rod sailed Mustang *to many victories.*

SHIELDS

LOA 30'2½"   LWL 20'
Beam 6'4"   Draft 4'9"
SA 382

A one-design class that incorporates big-boat
characteristics of seakindliness, stability, and
windward ability in a day-sailer

to bring Olin's name before a wider public. The customer was Rod Sr., who gambled $28,000, a goodly sum in the days of the stock market collapse, on building *Dorade* to Olin's design. From the start, and ever since, Rod Sr. has been a staunch supporter of his sons' careers. The father and sons had held many long discussions on the ideal ocean racer, and they all agreed that it should be something quite different from the boats that were then popular in the sport. Ocean racing was just beginning to catch on. There had been sporadic Transatlantic Races since 1866, mainly for large luxury yachts with big professional crews, but the revival of the Bermuda Race and Transpac after World War I and the growing interest in distance racing on the Great Lakes, where it had had a following since the turn of the century, were making quite a different sport out of it. The success of the 58-foot *Nina,* then considered a "little" boat, in winning the race to Spain in 1928 against big, professionally crewed yachts like *Atlantic* and *Elena* had focused additional attention on the sport. Most of the boats in it were husky descendants of the New England fishing schooners, designed to go offshore in all weathers, stay there, and come home with a large load of fish. They had been brought to their peak of development in John Alden's *Malabar*s, the dominant ocean racers of the era.

Able as these vessels were (and also fast when they got their weather, which meant something from the beam aft), Olin felt that a boat specifically designed for ocean racing as a yacht could do better on all points of sailing and in all conditions. In contrast to the beamy, stiff schooners and ketches that followed the fishing-boat tradition, he visualized a deep-water adaptation of something like the 6-Meter that was his first published design. *Dorade* was long and slender, only 10¼-foot beam, with fine ends and a hull intended to take to the water easily and buoyantly.

She was also intended to have windward ability in an offshore slop without giving anything away on reaches and runs, possible due to her easily driven hull. A Marconi yawl rig, a rather radical one for offshore work in that schooner-dominated age, was designed for maximum efficiency and ease of handling and to take advantage of the rig allowance then included in the Bermuda Race Rule.

The description of her in the Design Section of the April 1930 *Yachting* stated in part that she was reminiscent of craft built to the International Rule of Measurement (which favored lean, long-ended, racy hulls), and that

> the designer's idea was to produce a hull which would be easily driven with a small sail plan, a fast, comfortable and easily handled craft under all conditions. The freeboard is good; ends are moderate. The body plan shows considerable deadrise and very moderate bilges, while all the fore and aft lines, especially the waterlines and

Dorade, *the boat that made Olin Stephens' reputation,*
with her original rig, including bowsprit

Dorade, *modernized for her Transatlantic triumph,*
with a handier inboard rig

diagonals, are long and easy. The heavy lead keel will make up for any apparent lack of stability due to moderate beam and slack bilges.

The yawl rig . . . is excessive neither in height nor breadth, and it is well proportioned to allow fine balance under headsails and mizzen, or mainsail and staysail—in other words, reefing will be almost unnecessary . . . Her performance against heavier, beamier boats will be watched with interest.

And watched it was, from astern by many "heavier, beamier boats." In her debut she broke into a virtual schooner monopoly on Bermuda Race prizes, taking second in Class B, third in fleet, and a prize for the first boat with all-amateur crew. The next year, with bowsprit removed to give her a new compact "knockabout" yawl rig, she set the sailing world on its ear by winning the Transatlantic Race by the astounding margin of two days boat-for-boat over much bigger entries, and of course a whopping corrected-time victory on a seventeen-day passage.

With Olin as skipper and father Rod and brother Rod in crew, *Dorade* was taken on the cold, foggy, northerly Great Circle route, splitting with the rest of the fleet off Nantucket, and the gamble, which required great firmness of decision in face of considerable critical difference of expert opinion, really paid off. The way she performed, she almost certainly would have won the race on corrected time anyway, but her boat-for-boat finish was greatly helped by the decision. Characteristically, Olin had analyzed previous performances, felt this route had the best percentage chance for success, and stuck to his thinking.

She added a victory in England's rugged Fastnet Race, and so much publicity was given to these feats in the general press that the *Dorade* crew was given a ticker-tape parade up Broadway to a City Hall reception—a New York tribute that was standard in the twenties and accorded to such varying personalities as Gertrude Ederle, Lindbergh, and Admiral Byrd. No other sailors have ever been given the same type of tribute.

In analyzing *Dorade*'s performance, Olin had this to say:

I may still be wrong, but personally I am more convinced that a boat with very moderate displacement and beam is the only right type for either ocean cruising or racing. She is on top of everything; she never hits a sea, or gets hit by one, with any weight, and she is very easy on her gear and crew. On *Dorade* we didn't carry away a single bit of gear except our spinnaker halyard, which was rope, and has since been replaced by wire.

Of course, this type of boat must not have too much sail. With her shortened rig, *Dorade* is a much better boat than she was last year. The short rig is one of the greatest

*Baruna was the superboat of her day and twice won the
Bermuda Race. She staged many memorable duels with Bolero
under several owners for each, and on each coast.*

Bolero, *one of the most beautiful of the 73-footers,*
set the Bermuda Race course record in 1956.

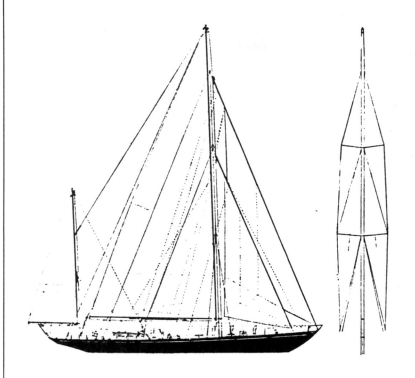

BOLERO

LOA 73'6"   LWL 51'
Beam 15'1"   Draft 9'7"
SA 336

An ocean racer in the classic mold

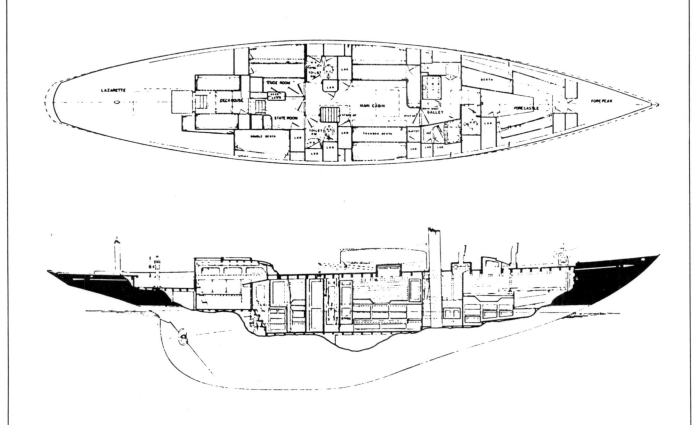

comforts. We seldom called out the watch below, as three fellows can keep a small rig working efficiently all the time. Any sail can be doused, set or trimmed more easily and more quickly when it is small. This makes for both speed and comfort.

If I had this race to sail over again, or almost any other ocean race, or if I were going for a good, long cruise, I should stick very close to *Dorade* both as to hull and rig, but I should give her somewhat more initial stability and raise up both her booms. I do not think that speed and comfort in a boat are qualities which cannot be readily combined, and I think that these changes would make for improvements in both respects.

These words from the twenty-three-year-old designer are of interest in the way they foreshadowed the string of S&S ocean racers that solidified his reputation during the 1930s. With *Dorade* as a base, he followed the same general vein in *Stormy Weather*, *Edlu*, and *Blitzen*, some of the more successful yachts of the 1930s that strongly built up his reputation. Interestingly, there were still enough schooner-minded people around for him to produce a schooner rig for *Dorade* (never installed, but published as a possible plan); another of his early successful designs and one of his first big commissions was the schooner *Brilliant* in 1931. She is now part of the fleet at the Mystic, Connecticut, Seaport. But his reputation was not made with schooners or with powerboats, though he has turned out many fine ones.

Stormy Weather, built for Philip LeBoutillier, New York department store executive, was an "improved" *Dorade*, and she compiled one of the best winning records in ocean-racing history. In describing her, Olin said

She is exactly what I think the rule [the version of the Bermuda Race Measurement Rule then in use] encourages. Her ends are short, beam ample, and displacement moderate. Personally, I should like her better with less beam, although she should be faster under the rule as she is. The beam and displacement are both slightly under the figures set by the rule.

Her yawl rig is based on *Dorade's* but has been worked out more from the racing angle, as we are going to try out a single working jib. The three spreaders have been adopted to make it possible to carry a small Genoa jib.

In the 1934 Bermuda Race, *Stormy* was a touted favorite, but *Edlu*, owned by R. J. Schaefer and sailed by Robert N. Bavier, Sr., was the overall winner. *Dorade*, with Olin and Rod sailing her, beat *Stormy*, too, by finishing fifth in Class A and fleet to *Stormy's* seventh in both. *Edlu* was 56¼ feet to *Stormy's* 53 feet, and their

Stormy Weather, *which made the Miami-Nassau Race*
her special province for many years, was a Dorade *development*
and a widely influential boat.

beams were 13 and 12½ feet respectively, but both were sisters of the Stephens stamp that was to become so familiar and influential.

Edlu gave Stephens his first Bermuda winner, followed over the years by *Baruna* (twice), *Gesture, Argyll, Finisterre* (a record three times), and *Noryema*, as well as innumerable class prizes and the course record-holder, *Bolero.*

Although *Stormy*'s debut had not been outstanding, she had impressed everyone by being the only boat not forced to shorten sail in the 1934 Bermuda Race. The added beam and stability had helped her, and her owner still felt he had a winner. How right he was was proved in the 1935 Transatlantic to Norway, which she won handily with Rod as skipper, again taking the northern route; in addition, *Stormy* later built up a fantastic string of victories in the Miami-Nassau Race and other SORC events. Rod in the field, putting his knowledge of boatbuilding and expertise with equipment to use, and Olin at the board—each concerned with careful attention to detail—had become the continuing S&S hallmark; *Stormy* served to dramatize the combination.

Bill Taylor, the famous Pulitzer Prize–winning yachting journalist, told the story of walking with John Alden through the Nevins Yard on City Island one day in 1935, when the designer suddenly stopped at a hull unidentifiable under her winter cover, studied the lines, and said, "In my opinion a better design would be impossible to achieve." He was looking at *Stormy Weather.*

After the 1934 season, Olin gave up racing his own boat and has hardly sailed at all for pure recreation ever since. He has continued to sail aboard boats of his own design all over the world and has been in on some memorable races that way, but his involvement has been strictly from the point of view of a designer keeping in touch with the way his boats act and feel, and with the latest developments from other designers. He is forever watching the way a boat moves through the water; the way the bow wave, quarter wave, and wake form and act; and the way the rig and sails look—always with an ever-analytical eye.

To get away from boats and to have a life and a means of relaxation that is personal and completely removed from the pressures of high-level sailing competition (which, ironically, is the "relaxation" of most of the other people involved), Olin has a weekend-and-vacation farm in the quiet, remote hills of northwestern Connecticut. It is not too far away physically, but in mood and atmosphere it is a few light-years removed from the typical scene of his design triumphs—the slashing, spray-flinging brouhaha of a starting line or the long thrash to windward in steep seas. A man of quiet, cultured tastes, he enjoys classical music, paints for

Finisterre was probably the most successful ocean racer of all time.

relaxation, and occasionally engages in tennis at a low-key level. The graceful hills and untouched forests of the countryside refresh him for a return to what amounts to a highly competitive and pressure-filled existence at the drawing board, at the conference table with the rule makers, and in consultation with clients and their highly personalized and demanding commissions.

With the many victories by S&S designs in the 1930s, commissions began to come in from all over the world, as well as from all parts of North America, until Olin Stephens' name became the best known of all yacht designers internationally. His name today is represented by almost as many foreign boats, especially in England and Scandinavia, as at home.

All this also led to another kind of involvement. When a second challenge for the America's Cup was accepted from T. O. M. Sopwith (the British aircraft tycoon who had come closer than anyone else in history to lifting the Cup in 1934 with *Endeavour*), Harold S. Vanderbilt, our defending skipper in 1930 and 1934, decided to go it alone in building a defense candidate, the only new vessel built in the Depression year of 1937. Once again he wanted to work with Starling Burgess, who had designed *Enterprise,* the 1930 winner, and *Rainbow,* the shaky victor in 1934, but he also decided that the brilliant young designer whose ocean racers had been causing such a stir should be included in the operation. It was determined that Stephens and Burgess would work together, each creating possible designs that were to be tank-tested at the new facility just being developed by Professor Kenneth Davidson at Stevens Institute. They would then combine forces on the final design chosen. *Ranger* emerged as the final design, and, though it has never been officially announced whose contribution carried more weight, Olin has led people to believe that the greater credit goes to Burgess.

This was an extremely valuable experience for the twenty-eight-year-old designer—not only working with the vastly experienced Burgess, but also sailing aboard *Ranger*. Rod, too, was in the crew as rigging expert, general acrobat, and troubleshooter, and the practical experience, plus the fame attached to being connected with this "super boat," enhanced the S&S reputation tremendously. Out of this involvement, Olin ended up with a commission from Vanderbilt in 1939 to design a 12-Meter for international competition. Vanderbilt wanted to campaign a boat in England, and the result was *Vim.* She cleaned up abroad, was obviously a great step forward in this class, and gave Stephens a backlog of experience that no other designer possessed when the 12-Meter Class was selected for the America's Cup competition upon its revival in 1958.

Super J boat Ranger, *in whose design Stephens cooperated*

Through the *Ranger* project and his subsequent work on *Vim*, Stephens became a firm believer in the tank-testing road. This was a relatively new "scientific" approach to sailboat designing and Stephens, Burgess, and Professor Davidson had a great deal to do with developing it. Tank testing of large ships was not new; they were towed in a straight line to test their resistance and wave-making characteristics. However, the special task of testing a sailing hull at an angle of heel and making leeway was something else. There were problems that could not be solved, such as the relation of a model-sized hull to the viscosity (i.e., thickness in breaking-up) of the water. Water breaking up along a waterline and forming into bow waves, quarter waves, and wakes does not have the same relationship to a model as it does to a full-sized hull at sea. Spray, droplets, and aeration are in very different proportion, so all the answers are not implicit in tank-test results. It was, however, a great advance over the "seaman's eye" and "rule of thumb" methods that had been in use for sailing hulls up to that time. Tank testing was eventually to become a major influence in the work of almost every successful yacht designer, and it has been of great importance to Olin, but he laughs at the tendency of some laymen to attach too much importance to the supposed magical properties of the process.

"You can use the results of tank testing as a guide," he has said, "and they can give you a certain amount of information on what you can reasonably expect in a finished boat, but the full-sized boat in actual sea conditions could still act differently from the indications of pure tank testing. You are never absolutely sure until the elements of design, sails, skipper and crew are combined."

On another occasion, he said,

> The results of tank testing alone are not the final test of a designer. If that were the case, we could hold the America's Cup in the towing tank and save everybody else all the trouble and expense. The hull that came up with the best set of statistics would be declared the winner.
>
> The criterion is still the overall effect achieved by the designer in the finished yacht racing on a course. The towing tank tests merely provide information from which to work. They are an indication only, a limited answer to how the boat will eventually perform.

The ability of the designer to put all this together in a boat at sea has been called "accommodating" the boat to the water, and this has been Olin's real forte over all the years from the first 6-Meter, so brilliantly brought to the fore by *Dorade*.

Baccara is a modern-day example of the big 73-footers. She was launched in 1970.

Columbia, *the first post-World War II Stephens Twelve,*
was the 1958 defender. Her underbody was conventional.

This quality of accommodating to the water has been a particular characteristic of his 12-Meter designs in a line of descent from *Vim* to *Columbia, Constellation, Intrepid,* and *Courageous.* When the America's Cup series was revived in 1958, *Vim* was still around as a starting point, and she had been thoroughly refitted and modernized as a candidate for the defender's berth. Going back to her design as a starter, Olin came up with *Columbia* after tank-testing various sets of lines in comparison with *Vim*'s model, and *Columbia* was just that little bit faster than her older sister. With Bus Mosbacher making his first appearance in America's Cup competition as *Vim*'s skipper, and with a crack crew that had months more of training than the boats built that year, the 1939 boat put up a stirring fight. However, *Columbia,* with both Stephens brothers in the crew, gradually put her potential together and won out in a hard-fought trial series.

In 1962, no one ordered a new Stephens 12-Meter, and *Columbia* was the only S&S contender, failing to make it against a revamped *Weatherly.* The 1964 campaign was one of the most dramatic selection series, as the Luders-designed *American Eagle* got off to a fast start, winning her first dozen or so races. Olin had turned out *Constellation* as a hoped-for improvement on *Columbia,* and she showed flashes of potential but she wasn't well organized. The Stephens brothers spent a long anxious summer helping to bring their brainchild along; they had faith in their design, and eventually, after some arduous analytical work and a delicate series of negotiations to get the best crew aboard, she really began to move. The series turned around dramatically in midsummer with Bob Bavier as helmsman and Rod as "second eyes," and *"Connie"* eventually gained a smashing victory in the final selection series and an easy win over the British *Sovereign.* There are many who still feel that she was as fine a 12-Meter design as there has ever been, though the theories of the years following seemed to outdate her.

In 1967, Olin designed *Intrepid* with such innovations, at least in 12-Meter design, as a rudder separated from the keel, a trim tab on the keel, and below-deck winches, and she was completely unbeatable in the selection trials and Cup matches. This was the first time that the formidable combination of Stephens as designer and Bus Mosbacher as skipper had worked together on a new boat, and it was a great team. In 1970, S&S got the contract to design *Valiant,* and the result was the first comparative failure in the string of S&S Twelves. She was quite a departure from the rather direct line of descent from *Vim* through the two C boats to *Intrepid,* with a very full-bodied after section and small rudder, quite heavy, and with a higher wetted surface-to-sail area ratio. Although she was in the fight to the end, she was the first Stephens Twelve to fail to make the defender's berth. *Courageous* in 1974 reverted to the *Vim-Columbia* line of descent.

Constellation, *a slow starter in 1964, finally triumphed*
over American Eagle *in the trials and whomped* Sovereign
in the Cup match. Her winches were still on deck.

Intrepid, *a runaway victor in 1967*
over all competition, introduced below-decks
winches and separate-rudder steering.

Running Tide *managed to remain competitive in the switch
from the CCA Rule to the IOR. She embodied much
12-Meter thinking adapted into an ocean racer.*

RUNNING TIDE

LOA 60′6″   LWL 45′
Beam 14′3″   Draft 9′
SA 1516

*Twelve-Meter thinking carried into an able
ocean racer*

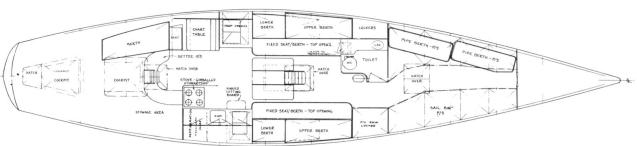

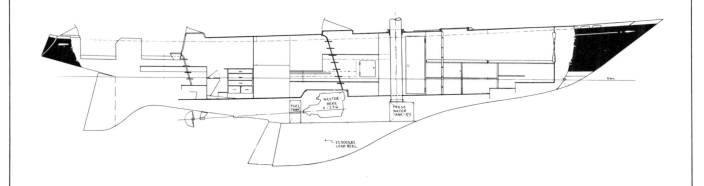

Above, a graphic demonstration of how much stiffer
Intrepid *(on left) was in the 1967 matches*
than the Australian challenger Dame Pattie

Right, Valiant *in 1970 represented a departure in thinking*
from the previous line of Stephens Twelves
and became his first new one that failed
to be selected as defender.

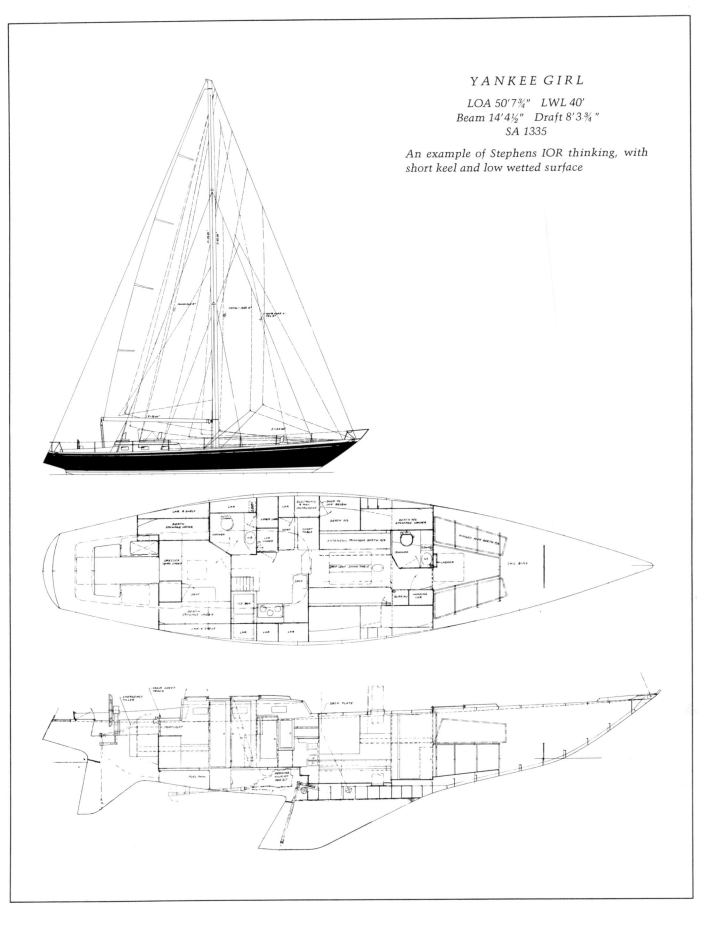

YANKEE GIRL

LOA 50'7¾"   LWL 40'
Beam 14'4½"   Draft 8'3¾"
SA 1335

*An example of Stephens IOR thinking, with
short keel and low wetted surface*

The great S&S success in the 1972 Bermuda Race—and in such events around the world as the One Ton Cup competition, the Sydney-Hobart Race, and the 1971 Southern Ocean Racing Conference, won by *Running Tide*—helped to soften the sting of the *Valiant* campaign. Olin is the first to admit that he is always learning and trying new theories, and that these new theories sometimes take him in the wrong direction. Also, changes in the measurement rules that have been in use over the years have necessitated changes in thinking too.

That his own theories and beliefs can be altered by having to design to a changing rule or to some special requirement has never been more dramatically demonstrated than by *Finisterre*, perhaps the best known of all his successful ocean racers. This 38-foot yawl came at a time when the Cruising Club of America Rule, which had grown out of the old Bermuda Race Rule, heavily favored beamy, shallow centerboarders, largely as a result of gradual penalizing of boats of the *Dorade-Stormy Weather* tradition because of their continued success.

Finisterre's owner, Carleton Mitchell, wanted to take advantage of the state of the rule, and he also wanted a boat that would be the "biggest little boat" he could possibly get for a combination of racing success with comfortable features for cruising and living aboard. Many of his requirements were not Olin's idea of the right thing to do, but they worked out the compromise carefully and the result was the most dramatically successful ocean racer in history. She is the only boat to have won the Bermuda Race three times in a row. She was indeed very unlike *Dorade*, with her squat beamy hull, shallow draft, and relatively short ends; but she had great sail-carrying ability, she rated very low, and she could handle all kinds of sea conditions, including the dramatic 1960 Bermuda Race storm. She was also beautifully organized and sailed; Stephens is the first to admit that a designer is fortunate when his brainchild is in the hands of an owner who knows what it takes to win the big ones—organization, infinite attention to detail, a crack crew, and the desire to keep driving hard at all times.

After a forty-five-year career, Olin Stephens can hardly be called a "brilliant young designer" anymore, but the fascinating thing about the whole art-science of yacht designing is that someone with his vast backlog of experience can still admit to having more to learn and to recognizing new avenues of exploration.

Not too long ago he said, in reference to this approach to his work, "There is still so much to learn from the refinements that are possible in so many different applications that you have to try just a few more ideas each time and hope that they do take you forward. Too radical a break from the line of thinking you have been following [and he could have been referring to *Valiant*] could bring about a surprising result, unpleasantly surprising, that is."

Following his line of thinking from that 1928 6-Meter to a modern One Ton Cupper, from *Dorade* to *Noryema,* from *Vim* to *Courageous,* and, yes, even to the lessons of *Valiant* has brought many interesting and highly influential developments, as well as its most dramatic success story, to the world of yachting. Finally, it has not failed to keep the dean of designers forever young in his approach to his very special trade.

Courageous, *the 1974 Stephens Twelve, was a return to the line of descent from* Vim *and* Columbia *through* Constellation *and the 1967* Intrepid.

Index

NOTE

Page numbers in **boldface type**

refer to illustrations.

Index

Photo Credits

Bahamas News Bureau: 64, 82, 84, 103, back of jacket

Peter Barlow: 63

Neal Beckner: 74

Beckner Photo Service: 134, 152

Bermuda News Service: 93, 109, 117, 122, 125

Blackstone Studios: 76

Albert Cook, courtesy of the Herreshoff Marine Museum: 34

Norman Fortier: 73

Kent Hitchcock: 151

Ray Krantz: 170

Howe Lagarde: 88

Edwin Levick: frontis-piece, 28, 45, 59

Laurence Lowry: 173

Frederick Maura, courtesy of Bahamas News Bureau: 72, 154, 178

Charles Mottl & Co.: 112

Fusanori Nakajima: 191

Kenneth G. Ollar: 85

Bill Robinson: 38, 56, 89, 108, 128, (top), 133, 136 147, 164-5, 184, 188, 190

Roland Rose, courtesy of Bahamas News Service: 111, 115, 142, 182

Morris Rosenfeld & Sons: 31, 37, 40, 45, 52, 69, 79, 104, 120, 127, 132

Stanley Rosenfeld: 50, 190, 194

Salant Studio: 148

Roger Smith, courtesy of Bermuda News Service: 166

United States Coast Guard Official Photo: 58

John Weatherill, courtesy of Bermuda News Service: 90

A Note About the Author

Bill Robinson has written fourteen books on the sport of sailing, including *The Science of Sailing, The World of Yachting,* and *Legendary Yachts.* He races a catboat on the Shrewsbury River, owns a 36-foot cruising sloop, and lives in Rumson, New Jersey.

A Note About the Type

The text of this book was set in Olympus, a film version of Trump Mediaeval. Designed by Professor Georg Trump in the mid-1950's, Trump Mediaeval was cut and cast by the C. E. Weber Typefoundry of Stuttgart, West Germany. The roman letterforms are based on classical prototypes, but Professor Trump has imbued them with his own unmistakable style. The italic letterforms, unlike those of so many other typefaces, are closely related to their roman counterparts. The result is a truly contemporary type, notable for both its legibility and its versatility.

This book was composed by University Graphics, Inc.,
Shrewsbury, New Jersey;
printed by The Murray Printing Company,
Forge Village, Massachusetts;
and bound by The Book Press, Inc.,
Brattleboro, Vermont.

The book was designed by Earl Tidwell.